THE NEEDS OF THE ELDERLY IN THE 21st CENTURY

URBAN INSTITUTE REPORT 90-5

Sheila R. Zedlewski, Roberta O. Barnes, Martha R. Burt, Timothy D. McBride, and Jack A. Meyer

URBAN INSTITUTE PRESS

Washington, D.C.

THE URBAN INSTITUTE PRESS
2100 M Street, N.W.
Washington, D.C. 20037

Library of Congress Cataloging in Publication Data

The Needs of the Elderly in the 21st Century / Sheila R.
Zedlewski ... [et al.].

1. Aged--United States--Social conditions--Forecasting.
2. Aged--Services for--United States--Forecasting.
3. Twenty-first century--Forecasting.
I. Zedlewski, Sheila R. II. Series.

HQ1064.U5N285   1990   90-12253
362.6'0973'0905--dc 20   CIP

(Urban Institute Reports; 90-5 ISSN 0897-7399)

ISBN 0-87766-481-1

ISBN 0-87766-480-3 (casebound)

Printed in the United States of America.

Distributed by University Press of America

4720 Boston Way
Lanham, MD 20706

3 Henrietta Street
London WC2E 8LU ENGLAND

URBAN INSTITUTE REPORTS are designed to provide rapid dissemination of research and policy findings. Each report contains timely information and is rigorously reviewed to uphold the highest standards of policy research and analysis.

The Urban Institute is a nonprofit policy research and educational organization established in Washington, D.C., in 1968. Its staff investigates the social and economic problems confronting the nation and government policies and programs designed to alleviate such problems. The Institute disseminates significant findings of its research through the publications program of its Press. The Institute has two goals for work in each of its research areas: to help shape thinking about societal problems and efforts to solve them, and to improve government decisions and performance by providing better information and analytic tools.

Through work that ranges from broad conceptual studies to administrative and technical assistance, Institute researchers contribute to the stock of knowledge available to public officials and private individuals and groups concerned with formulating and implementing more efficient and effective government policy.

Conclusions or opinions expressed in Institute publications are those of the authors and do not necessarily reflect the views of other staff members, officers or trustees of the Institute, advisory groups, or any organizations that provide financial support to the Institute.

ACKNOWLEDGMENTS

The authors wish to thank Raymond Scott Hacker for his expert research and programming assistance throughout the course of this project. His dedication to research quality was crucial to the completion of this project. Anne Bergsman provided essential systems analysis support in preparing the long-range population forecasts. We also thank Brenda Brown for her cheerful assistance in the preparation of the manuscript.

This research was supported, in part, by a grant, number 90AR0101, from the Administration on Aging, Department of Health and Human Services, Washington, D.C. Grantees undertaking projects under government sponsorship are encouraged to express freely their findings and conclusions. A grant from The Prudential Foundation supported the final editing and preparation of this manuscript. Opinions expressed in this report are those of the authors and do not necessarily represent the views of The Urban Institute or its sponsors.

CONTENTS

Tables

Figures

ABSTRACT

This study uses microsimulation techniques to project the
elderly population's characteristics, incomes, and needs
between now and the year 2030. It enumerates how the
aging of America will affect requirements for long-term
care, social, and housing services. These services are critical to the well-being of older Americans, and in many
cases, the availability and affordability of such services
determines a senior citizen's ability to live independently
in the community. Because matching appropriate services
to the elderly's need will require careful planning on the
part of federal and state governments, the private sector,
and individuals, this study emphasizes that society must
plan now for the requirements of the next century's elderly
population.

This report indicates that demographics, living arrangements, disability, and income will be the major determinants of the future needs of the elderly. It shows that the
increase in demand for supportive services is likely to be
greater than many realize because future increases in the
number of frail elderly, elderly with health limitations, and
elderly living alone all will exceed the general increase in
the elderly population. But this study emphasizes that
although many factors driving the need for services are
unavoidable, many are within our power to influence. To
this end, it describes a combination of efforts that could be
launched to reduce the incidence of disability, to reform
the service delivery system so that people needing help get

no more nor no less than what they need and want, and to develop financing mechanisms to make the purchase of needed services affordable for *all* older Americans.

EXECUTIVE SUMMARY

Although the "aging of America" is a well-recognized trend, how it will affect requirements for long-term care, social, and housing services is uncertain. These services are critical to the well-being of older Americans, and in many cases the availability and affordability of services determines a senior citizen's ability to live independently in the community. Because matching appropriate services to the needs of the elderly will require careful planning by federal and state governments, the private sector, and individuals, this is the time to consider the requirements of the next century's elderly population.

This study uses microsimulation techniques to project the elderly population's characteristics, incomes, and needs between now and the year 2030. It enumerates the factors shaping the characteristics of the future elderly population and explains how these characteristics are likely to affect demands for services. The study projects demographic trends and growth in real income levels under varying assumptions about future death and disability rates. It analyzes the service delivery system and how this system could be altered to serve the needs of the future elderly in an efficient and affordable way.

The premise of the study is that although many factors driving the need for care are unavoidable, many are within our power to influence. A combination of efforts can and should be launched to reduce the incidence of disability, to reform the service delivery system so that people needing help get neither more nor less than what they need and want, and to develop financing mechanisms to make the purchase of needed services affordable for *all* older Americans. The analysis emphasizes that the needs of the elderly are difficult to categorize and often involve a blend of long-term care, social service, and housing needs.

MAJOR MODEL ASSUMPTIONS

The microsimulation model on which this study is based provides a powerful projection tool. Births, deaths, labor force participation, and other economic and social events interact to shape the profile of the population, within the aggregate assumptions about future mortality, fertility, real wage growth, and unemployment provided by the Social Security Administration.

Because of uncertainty about advances in medical technology and about the emergence of new deadly diseases, this study examines the implications of two mortality paths. The first assumes that the decline in death rates will slow to half its historical pace, and the second posits that the decline will continue at its historical pace--a decline of 1.2 percent per year.

Similar uncertainty surrounds projections of health and disability. Here, this study also examines the implications of two possible disability patterns. The first is that the relation between demographic characteristics and disability rates will not change. The second and more optimistic assumption is that the disability rate for a person of given characteristics will decline slowly--at a pace of about 1 percent per year.

MAJOR DETERMINANTS OF FUTURE NEEDS

The study's analysis of the major determinants of needs of the elderly in the 21st century is divided for discussion into demographic considerations, the expected patterns of living arrangements, the projected levels of disability, and the probable income levels of that group.

Demographics

Population changes will play an important role in shaping the needs of the elderly over the next 40 years. In 1984 just over 27 million people were age 65 or older. If the historical rate of reduction in death rates is cut in half, the elderly population will reach 64 million by the year 2030. If the historical rate of mortality reduction continues, the elderly population will reach 73 million by 2030, more than 2.5 times the size of today's elderly population.

The age composition of the elderly population will be important in determining the intensity of need for supportive services. Until about 2010, the elderly population will become increasingly old. But between 2010 and 2030 the elderly population, on average, will become younger as the "baby boomers" enter their senior years. Even though the age distribution changes in the first and second halves of the period, the number of frail elderly (persons age 85 and older) will increase substantially throughout the projection period. The projections illustrate the likely dramatic growth in this population: *There will be between 8.7 and 12 million frail elderly in 2030 (depending on the mortality rate projected), compared with 2.5 million in 1984. Thus, in the optimistic mortality projection for 2030, the frail elderly population will be 4.8 times the size of this population in 1984.*

The dramatic growth in the size of the frail elderly population is one of the factors that will considerably increase the need for support services in the community.

Living Arrangements

Between now and 2030 the historical gap in mortality between men and women is expected to at least stabilize, and under the optimistic scenario it will narrow slightly. This will lead to shorter terms of widowhood for some women. But even under this favorable scenario, our projections show that there will be a tremendous surge in the number and proportion of elderly living alone in the 21st century. Although the number living alone will increase because of the sheer increase in the size of the elderly population, two other factors will increase the relative proportion of elderly living alone. Recent low fertility and marriage rates will mean that fewer of the elderly will have children as potential care givers and that more will remain single throughout their lives. High divorce rates of recent cohorts also point to an increase in the number of elderly who will be living alone. In addition, all factors indicate that unmarried elderly persons prefer to live alone.

These projections suggest the following trends: *At least 30 million elderly persons are expected to be living alone in 2030, compared with 8.4 million in 1984. Thus, there will be at least 3.6 times as many elderly persons living alone in 2030 as there were in 1984. If mortality rates follow the more optimistic path, however, there will be 3.8 times as many elderly persons living alone in 2030 as there were in 1984.*

This surge in the number of elderly living alone will exert additional pressure on supportive services as fewer of the elderly live with significant care givers in the future. That is, private and public services will have to play a bigger role in facilitating independent living among the elderly of the future.

Disability Levels

A crucial question for future needs is the disability level of the elderly. Under this study's high-disability scenario (historical mortality rate reduction with no change in the disability rate), the number of elderly with some activity limitation will increase from 4.9 million in 1984 to 16.3 million in 2030, and the number of severely disabled (four or more activity limitations) will increase from 1.5 million to 5.8 million. Under the most optimistic assumptions (mortality rates continuing to decline at historical rates and disability rates declining), the number of elderly with some disability will increase to 13.4 million, and the number of severely disabled will increase to 4.4 million by 2030.

These estimates of disability point clearly to the need for more focus on measures directed at preventing disability among the elderly. The level of disability (along with living arrangements and age) is a key indicator of the future need for nursing home care, suggesting the following possibilities:

- If current rates of disability persist, the number of elderly requiring institutional care will more than triple by 2030 (under the optimistic mortality scenario)--from 1.3 million persons in 1984 to 5.3 million persons in 2030.

- If rates of disability decline modestly, the number of elderly requiring institutional care in 2030 will be 4.3 million, under the optimistic mortality projection.

Thus, a sharp increase in demand for supportive services to allow the elderly to continue living in the community is certain. Moreover, whereas an increase in the need for nursing home care is inevitable, the increase could be reduced if successful policies aimed at reducing disability rates among the elderly are adopted. And, as noted below, further reductions could be made if formal in-home services were more broadly available to the elderly.

Income

Although the incomes of the elderly are projected to increase in real terms, average annual income growth is not expected to be as rapid as that experienced by the elderly during the 1979-84 period. Moreover, real incomes are likely to grow unevenly among subgroups of the elderly population and across the 1990-2030 time horizon. For example, the following possibilities are suggested:

- There will be particularly strong growth in income for the "young" elderly--persons age 65 to 69--retiring in 2010. This cohort, born just before the baby boom, benefited by the strong U.S. economy during the 1960s. This factor will have an enormous impact 20 years later when this cohort enters their 80s. For example, real median income for married couples age 80 and older will increase by 4 percent a year between 2010 and 2030, compared with 1.4 percent between 1990 and 2010.

- The effects of recent earnings gains for women, their stronger attachments to the labor force, and their increases in pension eligibility will be particularly evident in 2030. The incomes of unmarried women (including never-married women, widows, and divorced women), for example, are expected to increase faster than the incomes for married couples or unmarried men between 2010 and 2030.

• The reduction in Social Security retirement benefits that will begin in the 21st century, coupled with sluggish average growth in earnings, will dampen the growth in income for the elderly when the baby boom population begins to retire.

This study also shows that a significant group of elderly persons will be financially at risk in the 21st century. Despite expected real gains in income, unmarried women will continue to disproportionately fall into the lowest income groups. Moreover, financial risk will remain greatest when senior citizens are very old, alone, and have limitations in activities of daily living. For example, 70 percent of the elderly population most at risk demographically in 2030--persons unmarried and very old--will fall into the bottom half of the income distribution.

IMPLICATIONS FOR FUTURE SERVICE NEEDS

There is a continuum of disability and need across the elderly population. As older people experience certain limitations in their functional capacities, they require a range of different kinds of help. Yet the needs of the elderly currently are met by an overlapping array of service providers--ranging from the federal government and state and local governments to the proprietary sector, the voluntary sector, and the family--and services typically are provided by category of service need. Not surprisingly, elderly persons often have difficulty penetrating the eligibility barriers for each different program. Given the vagaries of program eligibility, it may be the case--sadly and ironically--that entry into a nursing home may be the "solution" to what is basically a housing rather than a health problem. Similarly, entering a nursing home may emerge as a "solution" to the elderly person's inability to manage a household alone.

Although this discussion of needs of the future elderly is organized along traditional lines of long-term care, social services, and housing, this review makes it clear that policymakers must consider the interrelated nature of the needs of the elderly. Fewer barriers to entry across program eligibility criteria could reduce the inefficiency and inappropriateness in the panoply of services provided to the elderly. Yet it will be difficult to develop a single "solution" to the problems facing tomorrow's elderly. Some of the risks and needs they face can be placed into an insurance model, whereas others are more difficult to treat in this fashion.

Long-Term Care

The current mix of public and private long-term care policies is not well suited to the needs of the future elderly population. The system attempts to deal with the effects of disability while neglecting prevention. Reimbursement policies remain institutionally biased, despite clear preferences among the elderly to receive care in noninstitutional settings. The long-term care system is fragmented and poorly coordinated with the acute health care system. Finally, the system relies on out-of-pocket outlays that become unaffordable for many Americans.

The population at risk for long-term care services is growing at a phenomenal rate according to these projections: *In 1990, for example, there will be about 6.5 million elderly persons at risk for long-term care services. This number is expected to grow to between 9.1 and 10.1 million persons by 2010 (depending on the mortality and health assumption), and to between 13.8 and 16.7 million persons by 2030.*

Several avenues must be pursued to adjust to the changing long-term care needs of the elderly. The place to begin is with efforts to prevent disability in the first place. As noted, even a modest decrease in disability rates will significantly dampen the need for institutionalized long-term care services. Very few health care dollars are devoted to research that could prevent or at least postpone the diseases of aging--of the $145 billion spent on health care for the elderly in the United States in 1988, less than 0.5 percent was invested in research (Carpenter 1989, p. 86).

Second, alternative approaches to care delivery must be considered. The focus here should be care in the least restrictive and least costly environment possible. This discussion reviews a variety of alternative care arrangements including cooperative care, the day hospital, adult day health care, the subacute care alternative, comprehensive outpatient rehabilitation facilities, transitional care, hospital-hotels, and community care organizations.

Third, alternative approaches to financing long-term care services must be offered. As the population becomes increasingly aware that the risk for long-term care services faces all elderly people and that current insurance mechanisms do not cover this type of health care, more will be willing to pay for long-term care insurance. Moreover, these financing strategies should allow the elderly to plan far in advance for long-term care services. Their incomes tend to be highest just after retirement and lowest when long-term care services are needed. These projections show that a broad group of the elderly are likely to be able to afford the cost of moderate long-term care protection (with no prior hospitalization requirement, inflation protection, and a 20-day deductible) purchased at age 65, but most could not afford this level of protection if they waited until age 75. These projections suggest the following: *In 2030, 48 percent of elderly persons could afford this type of policy ($720 in 1988 dollars), by spending less than 5 percent of their income on insurance. On the other hand, only 13 percent of the elderly could finance the cost of a typical policy initiated for a 75-year-old ($2,400 per year) with less than 5 percent of their incomes.*

This discussion also suggests the possibility of using home equity to finance long-term care costs, or, as also discussed in the housing needs section, to finance dwelling adjustments and upgrades to facilitate independent living. It also suggests a variety of supportive government policies to encourage private financing of insurance and to assist those who can not afford the price of long-term care insurance.

Social Services

Social services, with respect to the elderly, are intended to facilitate continued independent residence in the community and to prevent or to delay institutionalization. Yet, most social services today are neither provided through government efforts nor covered by private insurance. Rather, they are provided by other family members. Recent data document the limited availability and affordability of formal in-home social/health services (home-delivered meals, homemaker services, visiting nurse services, home health aide, and adult day care):

- In 1984 only 6 percent of the elderly reported using some in-home services, despite the fact that 14 percent had one or more limitations in activities of daily living.

- Only 30 percent of elderly persons who were living alone and had 3 or more limitations in activities of daily living received formal, in-home services.

- Many older people with health limitations reported that although they need help, they do not get any. Depending on their level of disability, between 29 and 64 percent of the elderly who needed help did not get it. For those who did get some help, most of the help (between 76 and 86 percent) came from relatives.

The future elderly are likely to demand and require a more coherent system of social services. As noted above, the number of very old persons, the number of elderly with health limitations, and the number of elderly living alone will increase dramatically in the 21st century. In fact, more than one-third of the elderly population is expected to have some health limitation (either in basic activities of daily living or incidental activities of daily living) in 2010 and in 2030. These projections show the following trends:

- Using the criteria that an elderly person living in the community with two or more limitations in incidental activities of daily living (IADLs) or one or more limitations in activities of daily living (ADLs) needs some formal, in-home services, the demand for these services will rise dramatically--from 5.9 million elderly persons in 1990, to as many as 8.8 million elderly in 2010, and to 14.7 million elderly in 2030.

- Contrasting these numbers to the number of elderly who received formal services in 1984--1.6 million elderly--implies that this service sector needs to grow quickly and extensively.

To meet the need for services and to prevent both "doing without" and unnecessary institutionalization, the United States needs a system in which social services are available independent of residence. Both private and government insurance mechanisms should be available to cover necessary services. In addition, support and assistance should be available to family care givers to prevent "burnout" and to enable them to continue giving their family members the care they need. The system also should be flexible enough to cover the gamut of services needed by the elderly. Ideally, social services for the elderly would be integrated with housing, nutrition and health services, and enrichment activities that cover their needs--both physical and financial.

Housing

Housing policy should be considered as a critical link in the long-term care system. Today many chronically ill or frail elderly persons are institutionalized, at very high daily cost, who could potentially remain in the community if less costly solutions were made available. Some of the key elements in housing policy include expansion of programs that provide support services to elderly in assisted housing, and support for modifications to dwelling units such as ramps, grab bars, and special kitchen hardware that help impaired persons use their homes fully, increasing their independence and decreasing the burden on care givers. Coordination among long-term care, social service and housing assistance policies is essential.

Although the projections show that the proportion of elderly persons who rent their homes will decline in the future, the number of low-income, very old renters will continue to increase. For example, this study shows the following trends:

- The proportion of single, elderly persons who rent will decline from 39 percent in 1990 to 21 percent in 2030, but the number of elderly renters in the lowest income quartile will increase from 1.8 million in 1990 to 3.1 million in 2030 under the baseline projections.

- About one-half of the single, elderly low-income renters will be age 80 or older in 2030.

Thus, the number of persons who will need some housing assistance is likely to increase in the future. Of particular interest will be housing assistance accompanied by support services for low-income, frail elderly--those who have limitations in activities of daily living. A variety of housing-based options that have potential include the Congregate Housing Services Program, in which supportive services are provided to frail elderly in existing senior housing or newly constructed congregate facilities; the Congregate Housing Certificate Program, in which households eligible both on the basis of low income and high risk of institutionalization receive a voucher to occupy a unit in a privately operated congregate housing project that provides independent living with the necessary nonmedical support services; the Housing and Support Services Certificate Program, in which all frail elderly persons who receive rent subsidies also receive subsidies for support services; and enrollment of elderly residents of assisted housing in a Social/Health Maintenance Organization.

This discussion also suggests that vouchers and reverse annuity mortgages (RAMs) should be made available to low-income home owners so that they are able to modify their dwellings to accommodate their personal needs. Various other alternatives embedded in the long-term care system also should be coordinated with these options. States now are permitted more discretion in providing support services to Medicaid clients as an alternative to institutional care. Although not many elderly persons currently are served under these options, better coordination of financial support and eligibility for in-home services--from programs supported under the Social Services Block Grant, the Older Americans Act, housing-based assistance options, and board and care facilities financed under the Supplemental Security Income Program–may enhance their success.

Success also will require appropriate eligibility screening mechanisms, ideally through a centralized screening system at the local level. Careful case management and tailoring of services will be central to cost containment and to meet the individual needs of participants. Moreover, copayments from participants, based on income and on the quantity of services received, will be advisable to offset program costs and to help contain service use.

Chapter One

INTRODUCTION

The aging of the U.S. population will present one of the toughest public policy challenges ever faced by American society. Even under the assumption that future improvements in mortality will slow to half their historical pace, the number of persons age 65 and older will more than double by 2030. At least one of every five persons is expected to be elderly in the year 2030, compared with one of every eight persons today. Demographic aging is likely to have profound impacts on American society. For example, one can expect increasing demand for all types of health care services and other supportive services that will allow the elderly to live independently longer. In addition, one can foresee increasing strains on the public systems that serve the elderly.

This is the critical time to begin developing a public policy agenda that will plan for the needs of the future elderly. This agenda should not take a "business as usual" approach toward finding solutions but should examine and seriously consider innovative proposals that will take into account the changing characteristics of the elderly. Nor should it take a "wait and see" approach, because we know with reasonable certainty what the future will look like. The agenda for the future elderly also will need to identify the potential roles of the key providers of services--the elderly themselves, their families, the private sector, and various levels of government. The real challenge for public policymakers, private sector managers, and others interested in the well-being of older Americans will be to identify the most important needs of the older population and to adopt responsible policies and strategies to meet those needs.

This study offers guidance for this planning. The characteristics of the future elderly population are projected here with a focus on how these characteristics are likely to affect future needs, particularly for the frail elderly. The first part of this volume analyzes how the characteristics of older Americans are likely to change as the elderly grow in number into the 21st century. Needs will depend not only on the size of the aged population but also on their health, the availability of other family members to assist the frail elderly, and the ability of the elderly to pay for services that will assist them in independent living. The first two chapters synthesize what is currently known about the determinants of these characteristics, and, using that information, project what this implies. Using microsimulation techniques, we project the socioeconomic characteristics of the future elderly population to the year 2030. The importance of demographic and retirement income outcomes are highlighted in separate chapters.

Recognizing that no one can say with certainty what the size of or characteristics of the elderly population are likely to be 20 or 40 years from now, we have varied two key assumptions so that a range of outcomes is predicted. These two key assumptions are the future mortality experience of the U.S. population and the degree of disability of the elderly population. These assumptions are as follows:

- The base-case mortality scenario predicts that in the long run mortality rates will improve by 0.6 percent per year. The second, more optimistic, scenario predicts that mortality rates will improve by 1.2 percent per year. These assumptions were adapted from those used in the 1986

Social Security Annual Trustees projections. Essentially, Social Security argues that mortality rates will continue to improve, but the Trustees' "best guess" is that the pace of improvement will be less than the 1.2 percent historical rate of improvement experienced during the 1900-84 period. The second, more optimistic, mortality scenario shows the effect of continuing the 1900-84 historical trend.

- The baseline disability scenario predicts that the rate of disability among the elderly, measured in terms of the number of limitations in activities of daily living (ADLs), will be the same as that experienced among the elderly in 1984. The second, more optimistic, disability scenario predicts that the rate of disability will decline by a rate similar to the historical improvement in mortality--1.1 percent per year.

Thus, the baseline mortality scenario combined with the baseline disability scenario is presented as the "best guess" projection in this volume. But policymakers will have to be prepared to face what might be the "worse case" scenario regarding the potential strain placed on society's ability to provide for an aging population--that is, people living longer with the same rate of disability as now. Conversely, they should be aware that improvements in preventing diseases that cause long-term disability may mean that strains on the system will be less than expected. Thus, the third scenario presented in this volume combines the optimistic mortality scenario with the improving disability rate projection.

The projections also show that many other factors will affect the ability of the future elderly to care for themselves. For example, sex differences in mortality rates and recent marriage and divorce experience will combine to determine the marital distribution of the future elderly population. The fertility experience of recent cohorts will determine the number of family members available to care for senior Americans.

Another question surrounds the future financial picture of the elderly. On the one hand, increases in private pension coverage rates and recent changes in tax laws that govern private pension plans will ensure that more of the elderly will retire with a private pension to supplement their Social Security benefits. On the other hand, recent changes in the Social Security system mean that the elderly will retire with relatively lower benefits than today's elderly. In addition, more recent cohorts of workers have not experienced the same degree of growth in real earnings as did their predecessors, the generation before the baby boom cohort. The chapter that discusses retirement income shows the likely growth in income for the future elderly, and it shows how various subgroups of the elderly population are expected to fare in the future.

The second part of this volume examines what implications these projections have for the future needs of the elderly population. The focus is placed primarily on the needs of the frail elderly. For convenience, needs are divided into long-term health care, social services, and housing. This delineation, which is helpful for organizing trends and policy options, masks the interconnected nature of the real-life problems facing senior citizens. The needs of the elderly are difficult to categorize and often involve a blend of the problems discussed in each of the three chapters. Policies designed to serve the needs of the elderly must be more sensitive to this overlap, and each of the chapters highlights this overlap. Each of the separate chapters discusses the current system but then discusses more innovative services that may better serve the needs of the future elderly population. Each chapter also discusses the sensitivity of future needs to the alternative forecasts. Thus, a range of possible outcomes is provided. The study does not examine the cost implications of the future needs of the elderly. Some projections of the elderly's ability to pay for long-term care through private insurance mechanisms are provided. But we do not attempt to project the costs of services or tackle the issue of who should bear the financial burden. These questions require a full treatment by themselves.

Chapter Two

DEMOGRAPHIC CHARACTERISTICS OF
THE FUTURE ELDERLY POPULATION

This chapter provides a demographic framework for the subsequent discussions of the future needs of the elderly. This framework relies on population projections into the 21st century that are based on a microsimulation model that accounts for a range of life-events simultaneously.[1] Although the aggregate projection outcomes are controlled to match the assumptions about future mortality provided by the Office of the Actuary of the Social Security Administration, the microsimulation model provides a stronger projection tool because it includes not only deaths, labor force participation, and other economic and social events, but also the interactions among these variables that will shape the profile of the future elderly population.

Forces shaping the projections of the elderly population in the 21st century are best understood by tracking the passage of the baby boom generation. In 1990 this large cohort of Americans--born between 1946 and 1962--will be entering their middle years. By 2010 the vanguard of this cohort will pass the 60-year mark, and by 2020 the cohort will dominate the elderly population. Only the oldest members of society--those 75 and above--would have been born before the mid-1940s. By 2030 the baby boom will be approaching advanced age, and some of the "baby bust" cohort will enter the ranks of the youngest elderly. The rapid growth in the overall elderly population will slow, and the population will once again grow younger as the percentage of people under age 65 will rise for a time.

Thus, to the extent that the oldest members of the elderly population require more supportive services to maintain their independence and achieve successful aging, the greatest strain on producing these services will begin around the year 2030, when the oldest members of the baby boom generation reach age 85. Moreover, the real peak in the demand for services will occur somewhat later when the majority of the baby boom cohort enters their 80s. Heavy demands for supportive services will continue until the baby boom generation passes out of the age distribution.

This chapter steps through some of the most important demographic forces that will shape the needs of the future elderly population. Death rates, of course, will determine the number of elderly who will be alive. The sheer size of the elderly population is an important general indicator of potential need, but the age distribution within the elderly population is even more critical because health and social service needs increase with advancing age. The movement of the baby boom cohort through the ranks of the elderly population during the 2010-30 period means that the age distribution of the elderly will change significantly during this period. Sex differentials in mortality experience will also be a potent factor in determining need, because this will affect the future living arrangements of the elderly. If, for example, the male/female differential in mortality rates narrows somewhat, a higher proportion of the future elderly will be married. Because it has been difficult historically to pinpoint future mortality experience, especially over a 40-year time span, this chapter examines two possible paths for mortality experience.

Living arrangements of the future elderly population also will be affected by their recent marital experience and by their propensity to prefer independent living. The baby boom cohort has experienced lower marriage rates and higher divorce rates than the current elderly population. Their fertility rates also have been relatively low. Thus, more of the elderly are likely to be unmarried in the future, and a lower proportion will have children with whom they might live. These demographic trends, coupled with what appears to be a strong desire on the part of the elderly to live independently, are likely to mean that there will be a disproportionate surge in the number of elderly living alone. Of course, this trend might be mitigated by improved mortality experience for men, because that would increase the proportion of elderly likely to be married.

Health will be another important factor in shaping the needs of the future elderly population. To the extent that the elderly have limitations in daily living activities, they will need to rely on supportive services provided by their communities, their families, or institutional arrangements. Current health characteristics of the elderly can guide projections of health, but here too there is considerable disagreement over whether the age-specific health status of the population will remain largely unchanged or whether future elderly will be healthier or sicker than the elderly today. This chapter examines two possible paths for the future health of elderly persons.

The final section of the chapter explores the dependency level of the future elderly population under each of the mortality and health scenarios. Current trends in institutionalization rates are used to project how many might require nursing home care, for example. The number of future elderly living in the community with either limitations in their activities of daily living (ADLs) or limitations in instrumental activities of daily living (IADLs) is projected to show that a continuum of services will be needed. These projections serve as the foundation for the discussions that follow in subsequent chapters on the health, service, and housing needs of the frail elderly population.

THE IMPORTANCE OF FUTURE MORTALITY

The aging of America is a phenomenon that has received increasing attention in the last decade. In fact, however, the population above age 65 has been growing more rapidly than the rest of the population for much of this century. In that sense, the aging of America is hardly news. From a demographer's perspective, however, recent and anticipated population trends are particularly interesting because the relative roles played by the forces of fertility and mortality have shifted. Historically, fertility rates have been the primary factor determining the age characteristics of the population, and changes in mortality simply have served to shape the age distribution "around the edges." In contrast, recent years have witnessed a return to a protracted decline in fertility rates, and mortality has become a more potent force in shaping the age structure, with net immigration potentially playing a significant role as well. Since the 1970s demographers' attention more often has focused on the dramatic declines in death rates, especially among older ages.

Although increased longevity per se is of interest, the fact that the elderly are representing an ever-increasing proportion of the total population is of more direct relevance for social policy. This phenomenon depends more critically on the pattern of fertility than on the pattern of mortality. That is, reductions in fertility rates have been equally important, or perhaps even more important, in shaping the demographic aging outcome most often highlighted. Whereas people over 65 constituted 9 percent of the U.S. population in 1960, they are likely to represent at least 21 percent of the population by 2030. Indeed, after the baby boom generation is replaced by the baby bust generation in older ages, the U.S. population once again will grow younger.

Although projections of population characteristics embody assumptions about fertility and mortality, changes in mortality patterns are of primary interest when the object is to look at the characteristics of the elderly population in future years. Fertility's role in determining the characteristics of the elderly population in the 21st century has already been played out, because the people who will reach age 65 by 2030 have already been born.

The Bureau of the Census and the Social Security Administration provide official projections of the population by age based on assumptions about the trends in fertility, mortality, and the level of net immigration (U.S. Bureau of the Census 1984; Board of Trustees 1986). The data on expected population trends presented below are based specifically on the assumptions built into Social Security's projections. These projections assume a slight, steady rise in the total fertility rate (relative to recent experience), reaching a maximum of 2.0 by 2010 in their intermediate forecast—a level slightly below replacement. Net immigration of 500,000 individuals per year is also assumed.

Of most interest here are the assumptions regarding mortality patterns. Perhaps inspired by the notion that there is some "natural" limitation on the human life span, the Census Bureau and Social Security actuarial projections often have underestimated the actual reductions in mortality. Indeed, death rates in the United States have declined historically at a rapid pace. Age-sex adjusted death rates fell at an average rate of 1.3 percent each year during the 1900-84 period (U.S. Bureau of the Census 1984, p. 18). Yet, many analysts feel that this level of reduction cannot be extrapolated into the future. Hence, methods to predict changes in central death rates have been sought.

Building models to predict mortality changes has been particularly tricky. Some researchers observe that demographic changes come in waves. During the years after World War II there were tremendous reductions in death rates across the age spectrum because of medical advances in fighting viral and bacterial infections. During the 1950s and 1960s the declines moderated or leveled off, sparking comments that life expectancy was approaching the unassailable maximum. These theories were cast to the wind again in the 1970s and 1980s, however, as medical science took further leaps in controlling deaths related to heart disease, stroke, and respiratory ailments. The lesson may be that advances in technology can never be anticipated with great certainty and that the power of changing technology can be quite great. Death rates from cancer, for example, have been rising, and there is great potential to witness yet another tremendous reduction in mortality if significant strides are made in this area.

The Census Bureau and the Social Security Administration have developed an algorithm for projecting death rates that is based on disease-specific reductions in death rates. Past reductions in mortality have varied greatly by the cause of death, and it is reasonable to assume that the future patterns will do the same. To the extent that unanticipated advances in the control of certain diseases are made, their projections may understate the actual declines in death rates in the years ahead. Analogously, to the extent that emergence of new sources of mortality have not been anticipated (for example, the long-run impact of AIDS is unknown), the declines in death rates may be mitigated.

Because of these uncertainties, it is important to consider alternative paths for future mortality. Two mortality paths were chosen for this analysis. The first is Social Security's intermediate assumption (Board of Trustees 1986, p. 81). This path assumes a 0.6 percent average annual mortality rate reduction, about one-half the average annual reduction experienced for the period 1900-85 (1.3 percent). The second path follows their more optimistic mortality assumption. This assumption generally continues the historical trend by assuming that the average annual decline in mortality is 1.2 percent.

The Size of the Elderly Population, 1990-2030

In 1984 there were 27.6 million people who were at least 65 years of age.[2] Under baseline assumptions, this population will grow to approximately 64 million individuals by the year 2030 (see table 2.1). In less than half a century, there will be approximately 2.3 elderly people in the United States for every person in that age group in 1984. Looking at the projections through time in more detail, the population 65 and older will grow from 32 million to 41 million from 1990 to 2010 (table 2.1). This represents a total increase of almost one-third in a 20-year span. By 2030, the elderly population will reach 64 million people, an additional 57 percent increase from the projected 2010 level.

Under the slightly more optimistic assumptions regarding mortality trends, the population counts and growth rates will be somewhat higher. In 1990 about 33 million people will be age 65 or older, and this figure reaches 73 million by 2030. Hence, the total elderly population grows by a factor of 2.6 between 1984 and 2030 in the optimistic projection, compared with 2.3 in the baseline projection. By 2030 there will be 8.2 million additional elderly persons, if mortality rates follow the more optimistic path.

Table 2.1   DISTRIBUTION OF POPULATION 65 YEARS OF
AGE AND OLDER UNDER TWO SCENARIOS,
1984-2030

Age Group	Baseline Mortality				Optimistic Mortality		
	1984[a]	1990	2010	2030	1990	2010	2030
	Number of Persons (in millions)						
65-69	9.2	10.4	12.7	17.9	10.6	13.0	18.8
70-74	7.2	8.3	9.0	16.5	8.4	9.4	17.8
75-79	5.5	6.1	6.9	12.3	6.3	7.3	13.5
80-84	3.2	4.0	5.9	9.0	4.1	6.5	10.4
85+	2.5	3.3	6.8	8.7	3.5	8.3	12.0
Total	27.6	32.1	41.2	64.3	32.9	44.5	72.5
	Percentage of Persons						
65-69	33.0	32.4	30.8	27.8	32.2	29.3	26.0
70-74	26.4	25.7	21.7	25.6	25.5	21.0	24.5
75-79	20.0	19.3	16.7	19.0	19.2	16.6	18.6
80-84	11.6	12.4	14.3	14.0	12.5	14.4	14.3
85+	9.0	10.3	16.5	13.6	10.6	18.6	16.6
Total	100.0	100.0	100.0	100.0	100.0	100.0	100.0

Source: Projections from the Urban Institute's Dynamic Simulation of
Income Model (DYNASIM).

a. Age distribution of the elderly in 1985 is approximated from the 1984
Supplement on Aging (SOA), a representative sample of the community-based elderly population, combined with the 1985 National
Nursing Home Survey, a representative sample of the institutionalized
elderly population, and 1985 National Nursing Home Survey.

The Age Distribution Within the Elderly Population

Aggregate population trends mask interesting changes within the elderly population. This group is far from homogenous, and its characteristics will be changing dramatically in the future. For example, the elderly population is becoming increasingly older. In 1984 about 9 percent of elderly persons were age 85 years or older; the proportion age 85 and older increases to 16.5 percent by 2010 (table 2.1). However, by 2030 this population will drop to a somewhat smaller share (13.6 percent) of the total elderly population, because the majority of the baby boom cohort will be in their 70s at this time. Hence, just as they have at every stage of their lives, the baby boom generation will cause a blip in the age pyramid. The elderly have been steadily growing and getting relatively older, but around 2010 they will actually start to get relatively younger for a time.

The extent to which this is true does depend critically on assumptions about age-specific death rates. As the optimistic projections show, if death rates fall sufficiently, the gains in population growth among the oldest old may mitigate against the "youthening" effect of the baby boom moving into the elderly population. Figure 2.1 illustrates the relative shares of the 85-and-older population to the total elderly population in both mortality projections. In the more optimistic scenario there will be 12 million persons in the 85-and-older category in 2030, compared with 8.7 million in the baseline projection. The difference in the age distributions between the two scenarios will be an important factor in determining future service needs. An increase of 3.3 million persons in the most vulnerable age group will increase future service needs significantly.

It is further illuminating to look at the implicit average annual growth rates for subgroups of the elderly. This

Figure 2.1   Elderly Population, 1984-2030
Age Distribution of Population, Age 65+

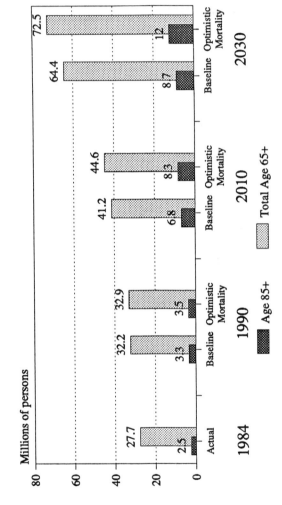

Source: Projections from The Urban Institute's DYNASIM model
and tabulations from the 1984 Supplement on Aging and the
1985 Nursing Home Survey.

Table 2.2   AVERAGE ANNUAL POPULATION GROWTH
RATES: BASELINE MORTALITY (in percent)

Age Group	1984-1990 (6 years)	1990-2010 (20 years)	2010-2030 (20 years)	1984-2030 (46 years)
65-69	2.0	1.0	1.7	1.5
70-74	2.1	0.4	3.0	1.8
75-84	2.3	1.2	2.6	2.0
85+	4.6	3.6	1.2	2.7
Total	2.4	1.3	2.2	1.8

Source: The Urban Institute's Dynamic Simulation of Income Model
(DYNASIM).

underscores the point that growth patterns among the
elderly are not homogeneous looked at from either a point
in time or across time. In table 2.2 the average annual
growth rates under the intermediate (baseline) mortality
assumptions are displayed. Between now and 2010,
growth rates for the population 85 and older are expected
to be well above 3 or even 4 percent per year. This is a
phenomenal rate of increase, viewed in the context that the
population age 65 to 69 is currently growing at 1 percent
per year. The greatest relative growth among the oldest
members of the aged is likely to occur between 1990 and
2010. This pattern will switch between 2010 and 2030,
when the greatest growth will occur among the 70- to 85-
year-olds.

These differences suggest that planning to meet age-
specific service demands may be difficult because of
disrupted growth patterns. A rapid buildup in systems to
serve the frail elderly will be imperative between now and
2010, during the period of most rapid growth in the oldest
old population. Of course, the absolute number of persons

age 85 and older will continue to increase during the 2010-30 period, implying continuing increases in service needs. Moreover, the optimistic mortality scenario suggests that preparation for caring for the most vulnerable will have to continue at a rapid pace for a long time.

Longevity Differences by Gender

The increase in the number of women relative to the number of men also will be an important factor in shaping the needs of the future elderly. As is well known, women live longer than men, on average. Historically, the difference between male and female life expectancies at birth--the gender gap--increased from 2.6 years in 1900 to 7.2 years in 1983. For 1970, the gender gap in life expectancy at birth was 7.8 years. It stabilized during the 1970s and has decreased slightly since 1979 (Wade 1988, p. 13). Life expectancy at age 65 for males increased from 11.3 years in 1900 to 14.3 years in 1983, whereas life expectancy at age 65 for females increased from 12.0 years to 18.6 years. The mortality assumptions used in this study predict little change (but no further widening) in the gender gap in mortality rates in the baseline scenario, but a slight narrowing of the gender gap in the more optimistic scenario. The life expectancy for males at age 65 increases from 14.5 years in 1985 to 16 years in 2010 in the baseline scenario and to 17.1 years in 2010 under the optimistic mortality scenario. Similarly, life expectancy at age 65 for women increases from 18.6 years in 1985 to 20.6 years in 2010 in the baseline scenario and to 21.9 years in 2010 under the optimistic mortality scenario.

Under the baseline mortality assumption, the ratio of women to men will be fairly constant in all age categories from 1990 through 2030 (see table 2.3). But under the optimistic mortality assumption the longevity gender gap will

Table 2.3   DISTRIBUTION OF ELDERLY POPULATION, IN
            SELECTED YEARS, UNDER TWO MORTALITY
            SCENARIOS BY AGE AND SEX[a]
            (Millions of persons)

Age Group	1990	2010 Baseline	2010 Optimistic	2030 Baseline	2030 Optimistic
			Men		
65-69	4.5	5.6	5.8	8.4	8.9
70-74	3.5	3.7	3.9	7.4	8.1
75-79	2.3	2.7	2.9	4.5	5.2
80-84	1.4	2.0	2.2	3.1	3.8
85+	1.0	2.1	2.6	2.7	4.0
Total	12.7	16.1	17.4	26.1	30.0
			Women		
65-69	5.9	7.1	7.3	9.5	9.9
70-74	4.8	5.3	5.5	9.1	9.7
75-79	3.8	4.2	4.4	7.8	8.3
80-84	2.6	3.9	4.3	5.9	6.6
85+	2.3	4.7	5.6	6.0	8.0
Total	19.4	25.2	27.1	38.3	42.5
		Ratio:	Women to Men		
65-69	1.3	1.3	1.3	1.1	1.1
70-74	1.4	1.4	1.4	1.2	1.2
75-79	1.7	1.6	1.5	1.7	1.6
80-84	1.9	2.0	2.0	1.9	1.7
85+	2.3	2.2	2.2	2.2	2.0
Total	1.5	1.6	1.6	1.6	1.4

Source: Projections from The Urban Institute's Dynamic Simulation of Income Model (DYNASIM).

a. Figures include all elderly (community and institutions).

narrow somewhat by 2030. For example, the optimistic scenario projects 1.7 women for every man in the 80 to 84 age category in 2030, compared with 1.9 in the baseline scenario, and there are 2.0 women for every man in the 85- and-older category in 2030, compared with a ratio of 2.2 in the baseline projection. The total number of women is 38.3 million in the baseline scenario, compared with 42.5 million in the optimistic scenario, a difference of 4.2 million (11 percent). Comparable numbers for men are 30 million in the 2030 optimistic projection and 26.1 million in the baseline scenario, a difference of 3.9 million (15 percent). The most pronounced increase in longevity for both men and women between the two mortality scenarios occurs in the 85-and-older age category.

Thus, the gender gap in mortality rates should at least stabilize, but it is also likely that breakthroughs in specific disease-related death rates (for example, heart disease) could increase the life span of men relatively more than for women. As discussed below, a narrowing of the gender gap will result in longer marriages and shorter periods of widowhood for some women.

FAMILY PATTERNS

The marital status and living arrangements of future elderly Americans will depend on their mortality experience as well as on historic marriage patterns. Women tend to outlive their husbands because of longevity differences and because they tend to marry older men. These two factors mean that women often live their most vulnerable years alone. But marriage patterns also affect this outcome. Divorce and remarriage patterns also affect the number of years that elderly women spend living alone.

Marital Status

The projected marital status of men and women for 1990, 2010, and 2030 is portrayed in table 2.4. As is well known, elderly men are twice as likely to be married as women. About 64 percent of elderly men are married in 1990, compared with 31 percent of women. This difference is related largely to the longevity gender gap and to age differences between spouses, but it is also because men are more likely to remarry after divorce or widowhood than are women (National Center for Health Statistics 1988, pp. 1-11). This difference between the proportion of elderly men and women who are married continues through 2010, but narrows somewhat by 2030 as a result of improvements in the mortality rates of men.

By 2030 the percentage of men and women who were never married will increase significantly. Recent marriage rates have been historically low, and this trend will influence the marital distribution of the elderly by 2030. Historically, the marriage rate per 1,000 population peaked in 1945 at 12.2 per 1,000 (U.S. Bureau of the Census 1987, p. 59). In 1945 the marriage rate began to decline, until it bottomed out at around 8.0 marriages per 1,000 population in the early 1960s. Subsequently, the marriage rate has risen, but it has never reached the 1945 peak. The marriage rate reached 10.4 per 1,000 by 1968 and has remained in that range throughout the 1980s--the rate was 10.0 in 1986. There has been a corresponding increase in the proportion of adults who are single in the United States. For example, 11 percent of men and 8 percent of women age 35 to 39 were never married in 1986, compared with 7.2 percent of men and 5.4 percent of women in the same age category in 1970 (U.S. Bureau of the Census 1976, p. 37). In addition, 22 percent of males and 14 percent of women age 30 to 34 were unmarried in 1986, compared with 9 percent of the men and 6.2 percent of the women in

Table 2.4   MARITAL STATUS OF PERSONS AGE 65 AND
OLDER IN PERCENT[a] (thousands as shown in
parentheses)

	1990	2010	2030
	Men		
Married	63.5	62.8	59.2
Previously married[b]	32.6	32.8	29.0
Never married	3.9	4.4	11.7
Totals			
Percent	100.0	100.0	100.0
Population (thousands)	(12,716)	(16,063)	(26,064)
	Women		
Married	31.0	30.8	32.9
Previously married[b]	64.5	65.5	58.8
Never married	4.5	3.7	8.2
Totals			
Percent	100.0	100.0	100.0
Population (thousands)	(19,447)	(25,151)	(38,328)

Source: The Urban Institute's Dynamic Simulation of Income Model
(DYNASIM).

Note: Population includes all elderly whether in community or institution.

a. Projections under baseline mortality assumption.

b. Includes divorced and widowed persons.

this age category in 1970. This trend means that more
adults will remain unmarried throughout their lifetimes
(Bloom and Bennett 1985). The DYNASIM model simulates
these recent marriage trends, and the result is a significant
increase in the proportion of elderly people who will be
single by 2030.

The stability in the proportion of the elderly population that is married between 1990 and 2030 is also noteworthy. The elderly population will be getting older during this period, but relatively more very old persons will be married. As outlined in table 2.5, the proportion of elderly persons age 85-and-older who are married will increase significantly between 1990 and 2010. In 2010 about 32 percent of men age 85-and-older will be married, compared with 24 percent in 1990. The percentage of women age 85-and-older who will be married doubles between 1990 and 2010--from 3.6 percent to 7.4 percent. The proportion of women who are married in the 80 to 84 age category is also expected to increase between 1990 and 2010, although not dramatically. The increase in marriage rates for the elderly reflects their improved longevity and the fact that married persons have lower mortality rates than unmarried persons, all else equal.

Between 2010 and 2030 further shifts in the marital status distribution of the elderly are expected. The percentage of the younger elderly men who are married will decrease from about 76 percent in 2010 to 68 percent in 2030. As the baby boom cohort retires, its lifetime marriage experience--higher rates of divorce and lower marriage rates--will change the marital status profile of the elderly population.

Nonetheless, both projections show that the proportion of women who are married will increase in nearly all age categories. Thus, for women, the long-run effect of recent marriage trends will be overshadowed by the improved mortality experience of their husbands. This effect is more significant in the optimistic mortality scenario in 2030, as the longevity gender gap narrows. The most significant increases in marriage rates will occur for the oldest age groups, because, as noted earlier, those age groups are expected to have the greater longevity increases (in relative terms). For example, in the optimistic mortality

Table 2.5   PERCENTAGE OF ELDERLY PERSONS MARRIED
BY AGE UNDER TWO MORTALITY SCENARIOS

Age	1990	2010		2030	
		Baseline Mortality	Optimistic Mortality	Baseline Mortality	Optimistic Mortality
			Men		
65-69	75.5	76.1	76.5	68.0	70.0
70-74	67.1	70.8	73.1	63.2	65.6
75-79	62.3	59.1	64.4	56.8	60.2
80-84	46.2	47.4	52.4	52.7	55.3
85+	24.3	31.9	34.6	33.0	39.7
All ages	63.5	62.8	63.7	59.2	61.2
			Women		
65-69	48.5	49.4	51.1	51.4	55.0
70-74	37.1	41.0	43.3	40.0	43.7
75-79	25.3	25.4	28.9	30.3	33.0
80-84	12.2	17.2	19.2	20.0	25.7
85+	3.6	7.4	9.0	8.8	11.6
All ages	31.0	30.8	32.0	32.9	35.4

Source: Projections from The Urban Institute's Dynamic Simulation of Income Model (DYNASIM).

Note: Projections under the baseline mortality assumption.

projection, the proportion of women age 85-and-older who are married in 2030 is almost 12 percent, compared with about 4 percent in 1990.

Increases in marriage rates for the very old in the optimistic mortality scenario will mean that a higher proportion will have a potential care giver at home during their most vulnerable years. This will not necessarily translate into lower demands for nursing home or other social services, however, because the total *number* of unmarried elderly persons is still considerably higher in the optimistic mortality projection than in the baseline mortality projection (figure 2.2).

Living Arrangements

The number of elderly who require social support to remain independent also will depend on the proportion of elderly *unmarried* persons who choose to live alone in the future. Research has shown a pronounced postwar trend toward increasingly independent living arrangements among unmarried elderly persons (Wolf and Soldo 1988; King 1988). Various studies have shown that the growth in personal income has had a positive effect on the probability of independent living (Schwartz, Danziger, and Smolensky 1984). Moreover, family size and disability have a negative influence on the probability of living alone (Soldo, Sharma, and Campbell 1984). More recent studies have shown that the sex and marital status of adult children appear to be important considerations in the decision to live with a child as well. Parents favor living with daughters, and they are more likely to live with their unmarried children, presumably because these children are less encumbered with competing demands of their own nuclear families. Home ownership also has a negative relationship with living with a child (Wolf 1984).

The question remains about how many elderly will live with kin in future years. Will recent trends continue? Or will the current rate of independent living among unmarried elderly persons continue indefinitely? Unfortunately, there is no well-established model of living arrangements among unmarried elderly persons, and it is

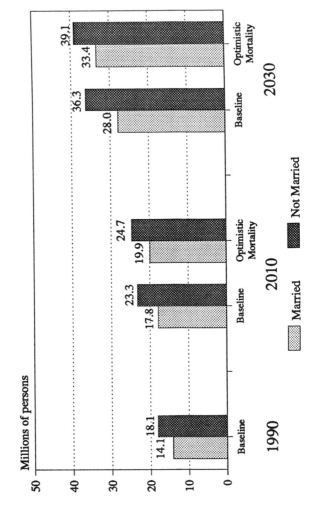

Figure 2.2   Marital Status of the Elderly, 1990–2030

Source: Projections from The Urban
Institute's DYNASIM Model

not a characteristic that is simulated as an integral part of The Urban Institute's Dynamic Simulation of Income (DYNASIM) demographic projection.[3] But, a number of correlates of independent living are simulated by the model, and these can be used as indicators of future trends in living arrangements. For example, the number of children ever born to elderly women often has been used as a rough indicator of potential kin availability (Wister and Burch 1983). Specifically, the number of children born to women has been a significant positive correlate of shared housing arrangements.

Recent fertility patterns will have important implications for the number of children available as potential care givers for the future elderly population. The mothers of the baby boom cohort had significantly more children than their foremothers (table 2.6). Women reaching age 65 in 1980, for example, had an average of 2.4 children during their lifetime, whereas women who will reach age 65 in the year 2000 had an average of 3.2 children. Only about 11 percent of women who will approach their senior years in 2000 did not have children, compared with 23 percent of their counterparts in 1975.

More recent fertility patterns will significantly change this distribution for the future elderly population. The birthrate dipped to 14.6 births per 1,000 population in 1975, compared with 25 per 1,000 population in 1955, the peak of the baby boom era. The birth rate subsequently increased to the 15.5 to 15.9 range in the 1980s (U.S. Bureau of the Census 1987, p. 59). The DYNASIM projections of more recent fertility experience are displayed in table 2.7. In the year 2030 women entering their senior years (age 65-69) will have, on average, 1.94 children, and 18.5 percent of them will be childless. In contrast, their more senior counterparts (age 85-and-older) will have had an average of 2.5 children, and only 10.6 percent of them will be childless. The DYNASIM projections also show that about

Table 2.6   NUMBERS OF CHILDREN BY COHORT AMONG
ALL WOMEN AGE 40 AND OLDER IN 1980

Years Cohort Reached or Will Reach 65	Percentage Distribution by Number of Children[a]				Average Number Children[b]
	0	1-3	4-5	6 or More	
2001-2005	10.7	58.7	21.6	9.0	2.94
1996-2000	11.4	52.7	24.3	11.7	3.20
1991-1995	11.6	55.1	22.0	11.2	3.08
1986-1990	14.1	57.8	18.2	10.0	2.86
1981-1985	17.2	58.0	16.5	8.3	2.57
1976-1980	22.5	57.0	12.9	7.6	2.35
1971-1975	24.2	54.9	12.8	8.2	2.29
1966-1970	23.9	52.9	12.9	10.3	2.44
Pre-1966[c]	21.9	50.1	15.3	12.7	2.68[d]

Source: King (1988): Percentage distribution of childbearing calculated from the 1:1000 Public Use Samples of the 1970 and 1980 censuses; average number of children for cohorts born between 1901 and 1920 taken from U.S. Public Health service, *Fertility Tables for Birth Cohorts by Color: United States, 1917-1973* (1976), p. 125; data for cohorts born between 1921 and 1940 taken from National Center for Health Statistics, *Vital Statistics of the United States, 1979, Volume I-Natality* (1984), p.33.

a. The percentage distribution of women by number of children is based on responses to questions about past childbearing by the subset of women in these birth cohorts who had not died before the 1980 Census.

b. The average number of children for women in a cohort reflects the childbearing experience of all members of the birth cohort who reached at least age 15, regardless of whether or not they survived to age 65 or older. In short, figures on the average number of children are simply the sum of the age-specific birth rates, from age 15 to age 50, for women born in the same years.

c. Includes only those women still alive at the time of the 1980 Census.

d. Average number of children for birth cohort of 1896-1900.

Table 2.7   NUMBER OF CHILDREN EVER BORN AMONG
ALL WOMEN AGE 65 AND OLDER IN 2030

Years Cohort Will Reach Age 65	Age in 2030	Percentage Distribution by Number of Children[a]					Average Number of Children
		0	1	2	3	4+	
2026-30	65-69	18.5	20.3	25.0	24.0	12.2	1.94
2021-25	70-74	22.1	19.0	23.4	24.7	10.8	1.86
2016-20	75-79	21.6	20.0	23.9	25.1	9.5	1.83
2011-15	80-84	16.0	20.0	27.1	25.7	11.1	2.00
Before 2011	85+	10.6	13.9	27.6	27.2	20.8	2.49

Source: Projections from The Urban Institute's Dynamic Simulation of Income Model (DYNASIM).

Note: Includes all women, community-based and institutionalized.

a. Children born to women age 65 and older, alive in 2030 under baseline mortality assumption.

22 percent of women age 70 to 74 in 2030 did not have a child during their lifetime, returning to the pattern of their foremothers who reached age 65 in 1976-80 (table 2.6). Thus, the potential for children as care givers will diminish for the baby boom cohort.

On the other hand, the apparent strong desire of the elderly to live independently may mean that the reduction in the number of children will not be an important factor in their choice of living arrangements. In a recent study, King (1988) shows that the historical trend in independent living choice for unmarried elderly persons is very strong. The proportion of elderly living with other relatives in 1983 was about 30 percent, and another 4 percent lived with unrelated individuals (King 1988, p. 54). But, if the 1960-84 trend toward living independently is extrapolated to the year 2030, King shows that only 13 percent of unmarried elderly persons would be living with other relatives, and 2 percent would be living with unrelated individuals. If the 1970-84 trend, which shows a slowdown in the shift away from extended family living, is extrapolated, King shows that 16 percent of unmarried elderly would be likely to live with other relatives and 4 percent with unrelated persons in the year 2030. The 1960-84 trends toward independent living occurred even though the proportion of older women with children was fairly steady during the 1960-80 period.

Thus, the number of elderly living alone in 2030 is expected to increase dramatically in both mortality scenarios (table 2.8).[4] The baseline projection shows that there will be about 12.2 million elderly persons living alone in 1990. Extrapolating the 1970-84 and 1960-84 trends to the baseline projections, the number living alone will increase to between 29.8 and 30.9 million by 2030, respectively. Applying these trends to the optimistic mortality projection, there will be between 33.2 million and 32.0 million elderly living alone in 2030. Thus, the increase in the number of elderly living alone is expected to outpace the general growth in the elderly population. In the baseline projection the entire elderly population doubles between 1990 and 2030 (64 million persons in 2030 compared with 32 million in 1990), but the number of elderly living alone increases by more than 250 percent.

HEALTH AND DISABILITY STATUS

The health characteristics of the future elderly population will be an important indicator of their ability to live independently. One measure of the health status of the elderly

Table 2.8 ALTERNATIVE PROJECTIONS OF LIVING ARRANGEMENTS FOR ELDERLY: EFFECTS OF EXTRAPOLATING RECENT TRENDS IN INDEPENDENT LIVING CHOICE

Living Arrangement	1990	2010				2030			
		Baseline		Optimistic Mortality		Baseline		Optimistic Mortality	
		Trend I[a]	Trend II[b]	Trend I[a]	Trend II[b]	Trend I[a]	Trend II[b]	Trend I[a]	Trend II[b]
				Number (millions of persons)					
Unmarried									
Alone	12.2	18.6	18.1	19.7	19.3	30.9	29.8	33.2	32.0
With relative	5.3	4.2	4.7	4.5	4.9	4.7	5.8	5.1	6.3
With unrelated others	.7	.5	.5	.5	.5	.7	.7	.8	.8
Married	14.0	17.9	17.9	19.9	19.9	28.0	28.0	33.4	33.4
Total	32.2	41.2	41.2	44.6	44.6	64.4	64.4	72.5	72.5
				Percentage Distribution					
Unmarried									
Alone	37.9	45.1	43.9	44.3	43.3	48.0	46.3	45.8	44.1
With relative	16.5	10.2	11.4	10.1	11.0	7.3	9.0	7.0	8.7
With unrelated others	2.1	1.2	1.2	1.1	1.1	1.2	1.2	1.1	1.1
Married	43.5	43.5	43.5	44.6	44.6	43.5	43.5	46.1	46.1
Total	100	100	100	100	100	100	100	100	100

Source: Projections from the Urban Institute's Dynamic Simulation of Income Model (DYNASIM), living arrangements of unmarried elderly persons imputed from King (1988).
a. 1960–1984 trend toward independent residence for unmarried elderly persons (King 1988).
b. 1970–1984 trend toward independent residence for unmarried elderly persons (King 1988).

population is their ability to perform the important activities of daily living (ADLs)--that is, eating, dressing, bathing, going to the toilet, and transferring (getting in and out of a bed or chair).[5] This measure is useful because it has been demonstrated that the elderly who have ADL limitations are much more likely to need health care and other services, especially long-term care services (Liu and Cornelius 1988).

The number of activities that can be considered the essential "activities of daily living" is a subjective list, of course. The ADL index discussed here is a slightly modified version of the index originally developed by Katz et al. (1970).[6] This index is perhaps the best known and most carefully tested of the various ADL indexes.[7] A broader ADL measure, of course, would indicate that a much larger percentage of the elderly population could be potentially disabled. But the shorter list of ADLs included in this study is becoming more broadly used because it captures activities that are most likely to be essential for independent living.[8] Moreover, it is likely that persons who are limited in the activities included in the shorter list of five ADLs are very likely to be limited in the ADLs included in the broader lists.[9]

Although the vast majority of the elderly (82 percent) had no ADL limitations in 1984, there were almost 5 million persons age 65 and over (including those living both in the community and in institutions) who were limited in their ability to perform one or more activities of daily living (table 2.9). As illustrated in figure 2.3, the prevalence of ADL limitations increases dramatically with age. For example, only 11 percent of the persons between age 65 and age 74 in 1984 had one or more ADL limitations, whereas about half of persons age 85 and over in 1984 were similarly disabled.

Figure 2.3 Disability of the Elderly in 1984
Persons Age 65 and Over With Limitations
in Activities of Daily Living (ADL's)

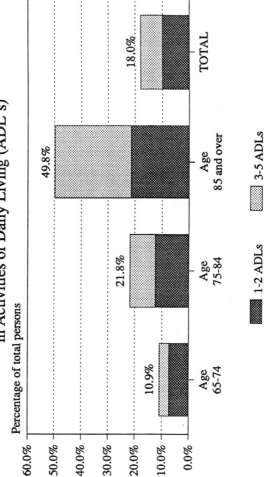

Source: Combined sample of persons from the National Health
Interview Survey/SOA and the 1985 National Nursing Home
Survey.

Table 2.9   LIMITATIONS ON ACTIVITIES OF DAILY LIVING (ADLs) OF PERSONS AGE 65 AND OVER IN 1984 (Includes persons in the community and institutions)

Activity Status	Thousands of persons				Percentage of total			
	Total	Age 65-74	Age 75-84	Age 85+	Total	Age 65-74	Age 75-84	Age 84+
No ADL limitations	22,560	14,555	6,775	1,229	82	89	78	50
One or more ADL limitations	4,911	1,806	1,884	1,221	18	11	22	50
1 ADL limitation	1,854	816	735	303	7	5	9	12
2 ADL limitations	970	400	345	225	4	2	4	9
3 ADL limitations	580	185	245	150	2	1	3	6
4 ADL limitations	783	242	285	256	3	6	3	11
5 ADL limitations	723	164	274	286	3	1	3	12
Total	27,470	16,361	8,659	2,450	100	100	100	100

Sources: Based on a combined sample of persons from: (1) the 1984 National Health Interview Survey/Supplement on Aging, and (2) the 1985 National Nursing Home Survey.

Note: The results are based on a combined sample of community-based persons in 1984 and persons in institutions in 1985. However, the differences in the institutionalized population between 1984 and 1985 should lead to only slight differences in the populations in the two years, suggesting that the results are a reasonable approximation of the 1984 population.

Forecasting the Health of the Elderly

Projecting the health status of future elderly is a difficult task. Not only do analysts disagree about the future trends in the number of elderly persons who will be disabled, but agreement does not even exist over the recent trends in the health status of the elderly. Generally, the interpretations of recent trends in the health status of the elderly can be summarized into three divergent viewpoints, each of which has different implications for the future.[10]

The first view is that the recent declines in mortality have been associated with similar improvements in the morbidity and disability of the elderly.[11] Under this view (sometimes called the mortality-compression model), the prevalence of disability and morbidity among the elderly at any given age should fall as mortality rates improve, because each improvement in longevity increases the proportion of a person's life that is spent free of disease and disability. The second view is that improvements in mortality in recent years have occurred by increasing the duration of time that a person survives with a disease or disability, so that elderly persons are spending the additional years of their lives in poor health (Gruenberg 1977; Kramer 1980). Under this view (sometimes called the failure-of-success model), the prevalence of disability and morbidity among the elderly at a given age should actually increase, because persons who would not have survived in the past are now surviving with diseases and disabilities. The final view falls between the optimistic first view and the pessimistic second view, suggesting that recent improvements in mortality have occurred because of the improved ability to manage the progression and severity of disease (Manton 1982). Although this view (sometimes called the dynamic equilibrium model) suggests that the elderly can expect to live longer, they can expect to spend at least a portion of these years either disabled or ill, because the incidence of disability and morbidity will not decline as rapidly as the mortality rate. If this viewpoint is correct, both the prevalence of disease and disability at a given age should increase as mortality improves, but the size of the increase should not be as great as the increase expected under the failure-of-success model.

Given the level of disagreement over the recent trends in the disability of the elderly, it is difficult to support any single method of projecting the future health status of the elderly. For this reason, two methods are used here to generate projections of the future disabled elderly population (as measured by the ADL index). The first method assumes that the best guess that can be made about the future incidence of disability is to assume that the rate of disability for a person with a given set of demographic characteristics will be the same in the future as it is today. The number of ADL limitations is assigned to each individual in the DYNASIM population, using a model that was estimated for this purpose and that was based on the representative sample of persons residing in both the community and in institutions.[12] The model results indicate that an individual's ADL limitations are significantly related to his or her age, sex, marital status, race, and geographic location. Using these associations, individuals are assigned to one of six possible levels of limitations on activities of daily living (that is, between zero and five ADL limitations). Although this scenario assumes that the relationship between demographic characteristics and ADL limitations will not change in the future, the percentage of elderly who are disabled will change as the demographic characteristics of the future elderly population change.

The second method used to project the ADL limitations of the elderly population uses the same model described above but imposes the additional assumption that the rate of disability for a person with a given set of demographic characteristics will gradually improve, at an annual rate equal to the assumed annual improvement in mortality.

The outcome of combining these two methods of projecting disability with the two alternative mortality assumptions discussed earlier is three alternative projections of the disabled population: (1) the base-case mortality scenario with no change in the rate of disability; (2) the optimistic mortality scenario, again with no change in the rate of disability; and (3) the optimistic mortality scenario combined with an optimistic health assumption in which disability rates decline at about the same rate as mortality rates--an average decline of 1.1 percent per year during the projection period.

The advantage of these three scenarios is that the projections can be interpreted as encompassing the three viewpoints about the trends in the disability status of the future elderly. The assumptions driving the base-case and the optimistic mortality scenarios are similar to the assumptions behind the failure-of-success model of disability, in that improvements in mortality are not accompanied by improvements in disability rates. On the other hand, the assumptions driving the optimistic mortality and health scenario are similar to those assumed by the mortality-compression model of disability, which assumes that improvements in mortality will go hand-in-hand with improvements in the health status of the elderly. If future trends in the disability of the elderly follow the dynamic-equilibrium model, the number of disabled elderly will fall somewhere between the projection that assumes no change in the rate of disability and the optimistic mortality and health projection, which assumes a decline in the incidence of disability.

Projections of the Disabled Elderly, 1990-2030

Given the base-case scenario, the number of elderly who will have ADL limitations is expected to increase by 123 percent between 1990 and 2030, from 6.2 to 13.8 million persons (table 2.10). The proportion of the elderly with ADL limitations will increase from 19.5 percent in 1990 to 21.4 percent in 2030. The population of elderly who are severely disabled (those with four or more ADL limitations) will increase by 137 percent between 1990 and 2030--from 1.9 to 4.5 million. Because this scenario assumes that the incidence of disability for an elderly person with a given set of demographic characteristics will not change in the future, these projections imply that demographic factors alone will increase the population of disabled elderly by more than 100 percent.

This rate of increase in the disabled elderly population is expected to exceed the rate of increase in the size of the total elderly population. Recall that the total elderly population will essentially double between 1990 and 2030 in the baseline projection--32.2 million persons in 1990 and 64.4 million persons in 2030 (table 2.1). A higher proportion of the elderly will be disabled because, as shown earlier, the number of very old (age 85-and-older) will increase faster than the total elderly population.

Under the optimistic mortality scenario, the percentage of elderly with ADL limitations will increase at a faster rate. The number of elderly with ADL limitations will increase by 163 percent--from 6.2 million persons in 1990 to 16.3 million persons in 2030 (figure 2.4). Moreover, the size of the severely-disabled population (four or more ADL limitations) will more than triple--from 1.9 million in 1990 to almost 5.8 million in 2030. In comparison, the projected size of the total elderly population in the optimistic mortality scenario will increase by 125 percent. The faster rate of increase in the disabled elderly population implies that the additional persons surviving will be those who are most likely to be disabled.

If the rate of disability follows a more optimistic path, however, incidence of disability among the elderly will not likely increase as fast. Under this scenario, the number of elderly persons with ADL limitations will be slightly lower

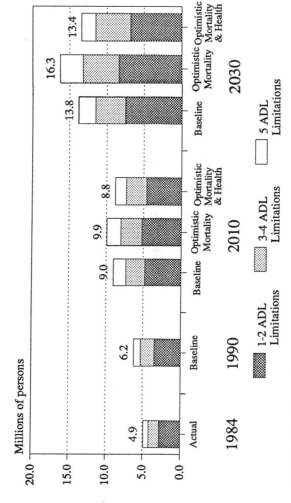

Figure 2.4 Disability of the Elderly, 1984-2030
ADL Limitations, Persons Age 65 and Over

Source: DYNASIM projections and tabulations from the 1984
Supplement on Aging and the 1985 Nursing Home Survey.
Note: Includes persons in the community and in institutions.

Table 2.10 PROJECTIONS OF LIMITATIONS ON ACTIVITIES OF DAILY LIVING (ADLs) OF PERSONS AGE 65 AND OVER, UNDER ALTERNATIVE MORTALITY AND DISABILITY ASSUMPTIONS, 1990-2030

Activity Status	Base-Case Scenario[a]			Optimistic Mortality Scenario[b]		Optimistic Mortality and Health Scenario[c]	
	1990	2010	2030	2010	2030	2010	2030
			Millions of Persons				
No ADL limitations	25.9	32.2	50.6	34.7	56.1	35.8	59.1
One or more ADL limitations	6.2	9.0	13.8	9.9	16.3	8.8	13.4
1 ADL limitation	2.2	3.1	4.8	3.3	5.3	2.8	4.2
2-3 ADL limitations	2.1	2.8	4.4	3.3	5.3	3.1	4.7
4-5 ADL limitations	1.9	3.1	4.5	3.3	5.8	2.9	4.4
Total	32.2	41.2	64.4	44.6	72.5	44.6	72.5

Percentage Distribution of Persons

No ADL limitations	80.4	78.2	78.6	77.9	77.4	80.3	81.6
One or more ADL limitations	19.5	21.7	21.4	22.1	22.6	19.8	18.5
1 ADL limitation	7.0	7.4	7.5	7.3	7.3	6.2	5.8
2-3 ADL limitations	6.6	6.8	6.9	7.4	7.3	6.9	6.5
4-5 ADL limitations	6.0	7.5	7.0	7.4	8.0	6.6	6.1
Total	100.0	100.0	100.0	100.0	100.0	100.0	100.0

Source: Projections from The Urban Institute's Dynamic Simulation of Income Model (DYNASIM).

a. Baseline mortality assumption: "middle-of-the-road" assumption from The Board of Trustees 1986 Report of the Federal Old-Age and Survivors Insurance and Disability Trust Funds.

b. Optimistic mortality assumption from The Board of Trustees 1986 Report of the Federal Old-Age and Survivors Insurance and Disability Trust Funds.

c. Optimistic mortality assumption combined with an analogous decline in disability rates (1.2 percent per year).

in 2010 and 2030 than in the base-case projection. Approximately 13.4 million elderly will have one or more ADL limitations in 2030 in the optimistic health and mortality projection, compared with 13.8 million elderly persons in 2030 in the baseline scenario (figure 2.4). Thus, even if the population proves significantly larger and older, this will not increase the number of elderly with health dependencies if medical advances are able to slow the rate of disability as well as the rate of mortality among the elderly population.

DEGREE OF DEPENDENCY

The demographic and health characteristics of the future elderly population discussed above will have important consequences for the future health and social services needs of this population. Of particular interest is the number of elderly who will be likely to require nursing home care in the future. As discussed later, increased demand for nursing home care is likely to place the greatest strain on personal and government resources. But the health and family circumstances of the future elderly also will affect the demand for care giving services that support independent living. Thus, one can explore current use of nursing home services to provide a *range* of baseline estimates for potential needs, but this need will be sensitive not only to the profile of the elderly population but also to the availability of health care services that might allow the elderly to live independently longer.

This section explores the likely degree of dependency of the future elderly population. Rates of nursing home usage in 1984 are used to project possible future usage.[13] Then the degree of impairment of the community-based population is projected using the ADL predictions shown earlier, and, for the elderly with no ADL limitations, the proportion likely to have difficulty with instrumental activities of daily living (IADLs) is projected.[14]

The number of elderly likely to require nursing home care will be very sensitive to mortality and disability rates (figure 2.5). In the worst-case scenario in 2030--historical improvements in mortality rates but constant disability rates--5.3 million elderly will require nursing home care. In contrast, about 4.3 million elderly will require nursing home care in the baseline and in the optimistic mortality and health scenarios. These projections illustrate the importance of devoting resources to health care and research focused on reducing the incidence of disability among the elderly.

As expected, the rate of increase in the number of elderly requiring nursing home care will be greater between 1990 and 2010 than between 2010 and 2030. This is because the baby boom cohort will have entered the ranks of the elderly by 2030, but none will be older than age 74. As shown earlier, the growth rate in the oldest old population will be higher between 1990 and 2010 than it will be after 2010. However, when the baby boom cohort eventually enters the ranks of the oldest-old, the reverse will be true. The greatest demand for nursing home care will occur beyond these projections, in the year 2040 and later, until the baby boom cohort passes out of the age distribution.

This point is illustrated in figure 2.6. The significant increase in the rate of institutionalization among the elderly will occur between 1990 and 2010 (from 5.6 percent in 1990 to 7.3 percent in 2010). In fact, in the 2030 optimistic mortality and health projection the rate of institutionalization among the elderly will return to a rate similar to that shown for 1990.

Current rates of institutionalization offer general guidance about the future need for nursing home care, and the

Figure 2.5   Institutionalized Elderly, 1984-2030

Persons Over Age 65 in Institutions

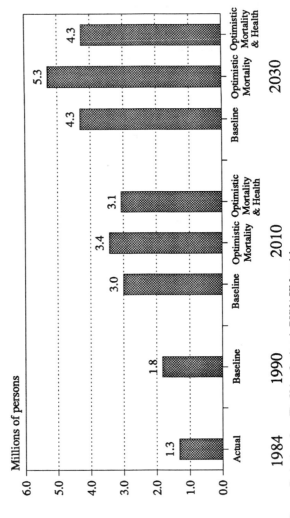

Source: Projections from The Urban Institute's DYNASIM model and tabulations from the 1984 Supplement on Aging and the 1985 Nursing Home Survey.

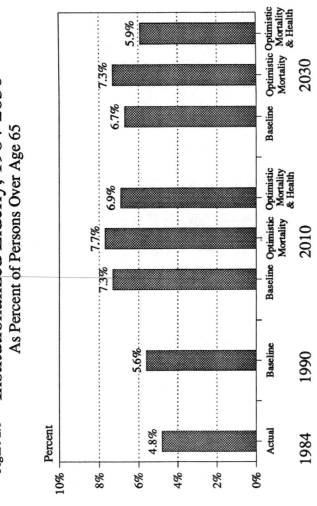

Figure 2.6   Institutionalized Elderly, 1984-2030
As Percent of Persons Over Age 65

Source: Projections from The Urban Institute's DYNASIM model
and tabulations from the 1984 Supplement on Aging and the
1985 Nursing Home Survey.

DYNASIM model captures the importance of changes in age, marital status, and health for predicting nursing home need. However, current nursing home rates also reflect the type of long-term health care services available today and the methods used to pay for these services. Some institutionalization may be preventable--for example, if more in-home services are available in the future and if there are insurance mechanisms to pay for these services. There is some degree of health and frailty, of course, beyond which in-home services would not be the efficient or appropriate mode of care.

The elderly in institutions will most likely be very old, unmarried persons with significant numbers of ADL limitations (table 2.11). For example, in the 2010 baseline projection, about 60 percent of this population has four or more ADL limitations and another 23 percent has two or three ADL limitations. If all of the elderly with zero or one ADL limitations were supported in their communities (no matter what their age or living circumstance), the number of elderly requiring a nursing home bed would decrease by 525,000 in 2010 and by 904,000 in 2030. Thus, the need for nursing homes potentially would be reduced by 17.5 percent in 2010, and by 21 percent in 2030. The percentage reductions would be somewhat higher in the more optimistic mortality scenario, because the proportion of elderly with none or one ADL in institutions is higher. There are relatively more persons in the 85-and-older age category in nursing homes in the optimistic mortality projection, and more of these persons could potentially be supported through community services because they are not substantially disabled. Thus, the importance of providing sufficient in-home health services will become even more important if longevity improves at the faster rate.

In 1990 about 11 million persons (34.3 percent of the elderly) will have some dependency (table 2.12). Of these,

1.8 million might require institutional services, 4.6 million of the community-based elderly will have one or more ADL limitations, and 4.6 million elderly will have one or more IADL limitations. The rate of dependency will rise somewhat after 1990, reaching 36.7 percent in 2010, as the elderly population grows older, and will essentially remain at this rate until 2030. But, the *number* of elderly persons with some dependency will rise substantially by 2030. About 15 million elderly persons have some dependency in the 2010 projection, and 23.5 million persons have some dependency in the 2030 projection. Increases in the degree of dependency will be even more dramatic if the elderly live longer and if their rate of disability does not improve (table 2.13).

Subsequent chapters explore the implications that these dependency levels will have for future policy. The expectation is that there will be a significant increase in the demand for supportive services that will allow the elderly to live in their communities for a longer time. Aside from the sheer increase in the number of elderly persons, a much larger proportion of the elderly is likely to be living alone, and a larger proportion is likely to have some level of health dependency. Even with additional supportive services, there is likely to be a surge in the need for long-term care facilities. An important element that will determine the supply of supportive services and long-term care facilities will be the elderly's ability to pay for these services, either through their retirement incomes and savings or through new financing mechanisms. The private sector could be expected to respond to the increased demand for supportive services for the elderly, if this becomes a profitable market. Thus, the future income profile of the elderly population is the missing piece of the total picture of the future elderly population that is explored in the next chapter.

Table 2.11   CHARACTERISTICS OF ELDERLY PERSONS IN INSTITUTIONS BY PROJECTION SCENARIO AND YEAR

	1990	2010			2030		
	Total	I	II	III	I	II	III
				Numbers (in thousands)				
Total	1,820	2,990	3,440	3,060	4,300	5,300	4,250
By number of ADLs							
0	170	210	260	250	310	350	390
1	240	310	390	360	590	590	500
2-3	420	670	800	800	880	1,210	1,090
4-5	990	1,800	1,990	1,650	2,520	3,150	2,270
By age							
65-74	200	303	308	283	578	476	375
75-79	340	382	328	296	718	723	554
80-84	350	558	525	464	685	845	693
85+	930	1,753	2,266	2,020	2,328	3,249	2,636
By sex							
Male	530	837	945	841	1,166	1,471	1,214
Female	1,290	2,159	2,483	2,221	3,144	3,823	3,045
By marital status							
Married	140	291	337	300	402	532	393
Not married	1,680	2,705	3,041	2,762	3,908	4,762	3,866

Percentage Distribution

By number of ADLs							
0	9.3	7.1	7.4	8.3	7.2	6.5	9.2
1	13.2	10.4	11.4	11.7	13.7	11.2	11.8
2-3	23.1	22.5	23.2	26.0	20.5	22.8	25.6
4-5	54.4	60.0	58.0	54.0	58.6	59.5	53.4
By age							
65-74	11.0	10.1	9.0	9.3	13.4	9.0	8.8
75-79	18.7	12.7	9.6	9.7	16.7	13.7	13.0
80-84	19.2	18.6	15.3	15.2	15.9	16.0	16.3
85+	51.0	58.5	66.1	66.0	54.1	61.4	61.9
By sex							
Male	29.1	27.9	27.5	27.5	27.0	27.8	28.5
Female	70.9	72.1	72.5	72.5	73.0	72.2	71.5
By marital status							
Married	7.7	9.7	9.8	9.8	9.3	10.1	9.2
Not married	92.3	90.3	90.2	90.2	90.7	89.9	90.8

Source: The Urban Institute's Dynamic Simulation of Income Model (DYNASIM).

Note: Projection scenarios are as follows: I Baseline Projection, II Optimistic Mortality, III Optimistic Mortality and Health.

Table 2.12   PREVALENCE OF DEPENDENCY AMONG THE ELDERLY: BASELINE PROJECTIONS 1990-2030   (thousands of persons)

| | Total Elderly | Total Elderly with Some Dependency[a] | | Persons with Some Type of Dependency | | |
| | | | | | Community-Based | |
	Total Elderly	Number	% of Elderly	Institu- tionalized	w/ADL Limitations[b]	w/IADL Limitations[c]
			1990			
65-69	10,430	2,240	21.5	80	980	1,180
70-74	8,260	2,170	26.2	120	890	1,160
75-79	6,180	2,340	37.9	340	1,020	980
80-84	3,970	1,940	49.0	350	880	710
85+	3,340	2,360	70.6	920	870	560
Total	32,160	11,050	34.3	1,820	4,640	4,590

2010

Age	Total	[a]	Percent		[b]	[c]
65-69	12,730	2,740	21.5	180	1,120	1,450
70-74	8,950	2,400	26.8	130	1,030	1,250
75-79	6,880	2,520	36.7	380	1,030	1,050
80-84	5,850	2,860	48.9	560	1,250	1,090
85+	6,800	4,610	67.8	1,750	1,770	1,090
Total	41,210	15,130	36.7	3,000	6,200	6,050

2030

Age	Total	[a]	Percent		[b]	[c]
65-69	17,940	3,900	21.7	240	1,630	2,030
70-74	16,500	4,620	28.0	340	2,020	2,260
75-79	12,240	4,600	37.5	720	1,930	1,950
80-84	8,970	4,240	47.3	690	1,890	1,660
85+	8,750	6,130	70.0	2,330	2,310	1,490
Total	64,400	23,490	36.5	4,320	9,770	9,400

Source: Projections from the Dynamic Simulation of Income Model (DYNASIM).

a. Total with some dependency includes institutionalized elderly and community-based elderly with ADL or IADL limitations.
b. Persons with limitations in Activities of Daily Living (ADLs).
c. Persons with difficulty with Instrumental Activities of Daily Living (IADL), but no ADL limitations.

Table 2.13   PREVALENCE OF DEPENDENCY AMONG THE ELDERLY UNDER ALTERNATIVE MORTALITY AND HEALTH ASSUMPTIONS: 2010 AND 2030 (thousands of persons)

| | Total Elderly | Total Elderly with Some Dependency[a] | | Persons with Some Type of Dependency | | |
| | | | | | Community-Based | |
		Number	% of Elderly	Institu-tionalized	ADL Dependent[b]	IADL Dependent[c]
2010: Optimistic Mortality with Baseline Health						
65-69	13,050	2,830	21.7	140	1,200	1,480
70-74	9,370	2,440	26.0	160	950	1,320
75-79	7,380	2,610	35.4	330	1,060	1,220
80-84	6,450	3,060	47.4	530	1,340	1,190
85+	8,320	5,830	70.1	2,270	2,140	1,420
Total	44,560	16,750	37.6	3,430	6,690	6,630
2010: Optimistic Mortality and Health						
65-69	13,050	2,640	20.2	130	1,000	1,510
70-74	9,370	2,350	25.1	160	860	1,340
75-79	7,380	2,440	33.1	300	890	1,260
80-84	6,450	2,890	44.8	460	1,180	1,250
85+	8,320	5,620	67.5	2,020	2,060	1,540
Total	44,560	15,940	35.8	3,060	5,990	6,890

2030: Optimistic Mortality with Baseline Health

65-69	18,820	4,100	21.8	170	1,800	2,130
70-74	17,760	4,850	27.3	310	2,090	2,450
75-79	13,540	4,940	36.5	720	2,010	2,200
80-84	10,400	5,000	48.1	850	2,250	1,900
85+	11,990	8,510	71.0	3,250	3,280	1,980
Total	72,500	27,390	37.8	5,290	11,430	10,660

2030: Optimistic Mortality and Health

65-69	18,820	3,730	19.8	140	1,410	2,180
70-74	17,760	4,420	24.9	240	1,640	2,540
75-79	13,540	4,540	33.5	550	1,690	2,300
80-84	10,400	4,590	44.1	690	1,850	2,050
85+	11,990	7,890	65.8	2,640	2,910	2,340
Total	72,500	25,150	34.7	4,260	9,500	11,400

Source: Projections from The Urban Institute's Dynamic Simulation of Income Model (DYNASIM).

a. Total with some dependency includes institutionalized elderly and community-based elderly with ADL or IADL limitations.
b. Persons with limitations in Activities of Daily Living (ADLs).
c. Persons with difficulty with Instrumental Activities of Daily Living (IADL), but no ADL limitations.

Notes, chapter two

1. This model, called the Dynamic Simulation of Income Model (DYNASIM), has been under development at The Urban Institute over the last twenty years. The model ages a Current Population Survey by simulating life events on a person and family level. The basic model includes fertility, mortality, marriage, divorce, education, labor force participation, hours of work, unemployment, and earnings. Each model incorporates behavioral equations that simulate differences in these life events by important socioeconomic factors such as age, race, sex, and income. It is fully described in Wertheimer and Zedlewski (1984). The history of the model's development is described in Zedlewski (1990).

2. This is an estimate of the total elderly population, including the elderly living in the community (from the Supplement on Aging) and the nursing hpome population (from the 1984 National Nursing Home Survey).

3. Wolf and Soldo (1988) provide a very useful model that predicts living arrangements, but this model only pertains to older women. In addition, since income is the strongest predictor of living independently in their model, further research would be needed to test the stability of the income coefficient over time before it could be used in DYNASIM.

4. The effect of using these probabilities to project ihe number of elderly living alone from the DYNASIM marital status projections is illustrated in table 2.8. That is, the percent of unmarried persons who would be likely to live with children or other persons was computed from King (1988), and these probabilities were applied to the DYNASIM marital status distributions.

5. The ADL index measures the disability level of the elderly, but it is only one of a number of possible measures of health status. Other possible measures of disability include self-reported health status, measures of work disability, and

measures of bedridden and activity-restricted days. In addition, health status could be measured by an index describing the morbidity of the elderly (i.e., the prevalence of certain diseases, including cancer, strokes, respiratory ailments, and Alzheimer's disease).

6. The ADL index used here differs from the Katz index in the exclusion of continence as an ADL. Continence was excluded for several reasons. First, incontinence is a difficulty that does not seem as severe as the other five ADLs. Second, over two-thirds of elderly persons with continence problems also were identified as having difficulty going to the toilet, suggesting that the fuller index of six ADLs may include some double-counting. Finally, current legislative proposals that use the ADL index as a guide for policy intervention are using the restricted list of five ADLs.

7. Other ADL indices include one used by Dawson et al. (1987), which combines the five ADLs included in the Katz index with walking and going outside. In other studies, the ADL index has included other combinations of ADLs.

8. Some studies restrict the ADL definition further by counting persons as disabled only if they report that they "require assistance" with the ADL, rather than that they "have difficulty" with the ADL, the definition used here.

9. For example, a person who has difficulty transferring is very likely to have difficulty walking or going outside, the two additional ADLs included in the Dawson index.

10. For a longer discussion and fuller comparison of these views, see either Chapman, LaPlante, and Wilensky (1986) or Ycas (1987).

11. This view has been taken by Fries (1980, 1983). Ycas (1987), using the National Health Interview Survey to look at recent trends, finds some evidence to suggest that the health status of the elderly improved in recent years. However, he is cautious

about the ability to use this evidence to support any projection of further improvements.

12. An ordered probit model was estimated to assign elderly persons to various ADL categories. A full description of this model is given in McBride and Hacker (1989). It is important to note that ADLs are imputed to the population forecasted by the DYNASIM model with no allowance for interactions between ADL limitations and other factors built into the model, except that these factors are in fact functions of the same set of demographic characteristics that drive the ADL model.

13. The probability of nursing home use is a point estimate, based on the characteristics of elderly in nursing homes in 1984. A data set representative of the entire elderly population in 1984 was built by combining the representative sample of the community-based elderly population from the 1984 Supplement on Aging and a representative sample of the nursing home population from the 1984 National Nursing Home Survey. Probabilities of institutionalization were estimated for separate ADL, sex, age, marital status categories, and these probabilities were used to project the number of elderly likely to be institutionalized in the DYNASIM projections.

14. IADL limitations include difficulty with preparing meals, going shopping, handling money, using the telephone, doing housework. The probability of having one or more limitations in IADLs was estimated from the Supplement on Aging to the National Health Interview Survey. The probability varies by ADL and age.

Chapter Three

INCOME CHARACTERISTICS OF THE FUTURE ELDERLY POPULATION

The fact that the income of the elderly population has increased significantly in recent years is well known. Real median income for families headed by persons age 65 and older increased by 69 percent between 1964 and 1984 (Radner 1987, p. 4). The incidence of poverty among elderly persons also has fallen dramatically. In 1966 the poverty rate for all elderly persons was 29 percent, compared with just over 12 percent in 1987 (Committee on Ways and Means 1989, p. 915).

During this period several factors helped to improve the incomes of older Americans. Federal policies enacted during the late 1960s and the early 1970s helped to break the strong link between poverty and old age that had existed in the United States. Between 1968 and 1973, for example, Social Security benefits rose faster than at any other time in the history of the program (Burkhauser and Duncan 1988). In 1974 the federal Supplemental Security Income (SSI) was implemented to provide a floor of income for the elderly, and full inflation indexing of Social Security benefits began. Private pensions also helped to boost the real incomes of older Americans as pension eligibility became increasingly common during this period. Finally, increases in real interest rates after the late 1960s significantly increased the incomes of the elderly with financial assets.[1]

This chapter explores what might be expected for future income levels of the elderly. Current earnings patterns, rates of accumulation of pension credits, and Social Security policy can be used to form a general picture of the future income of the elderly. Of course, these projections indicate what is likely to happen, should public policy and the economy stay on a fairly steady course. Just as in the past, however, policies affecting the income of the elderly may change significantly. For this reason, the discussion outlines general outcomes but then explores some of the uncertainties regarding the future.

Recent income and retirement savings patterns also can be used to examine the distribution of income among the future elderly population. The current distribution of income among the elderly is quite skewed. Although some of the elderly have accumulated significant sums of assets and pension benefits, many others exist on a more modest retirement income composed primarily of Social Security benefits. In addition, there are significant disparities in income by age and sex. Recent retirees are typically much better off than their older counterparts because real Social Security benefits tend to rise with each successive cohort's earnings levels, because private pension benefits are not indexed to inflation, and because some elderly spend down their assets to maintain their preretirement standard of living. Current income disparities by sex among the elderly are significant--the median income for unmarried women age 65 and older in 1986 was 80 percent of the median income for unmarried men (Grad 1988, p. 36). Labor force patterns of younger cohorts of women, however, should improve their future retirement incomes and narrow this gap. Thus, the discussion pays close attention to changes in these patterns expected for the future elderly population.

THE CHANGE IN REAL INCOME, 1990-2030

Real incomes of the elderly will continue to rise between 1990 and 2030 (table 3.1). But real income growth is likely to be uneven among subgroups of the elderly population and across time. These differences reflect some of the important demographic changes among these subgroups, changes in Social Security and private pension policies, and changes in the labor force participation and earnings among women.

For example, between 1990 and 2010 married couples' incomes will increase more rapidly than incomes for unmarried men or women, but the reverse is true between 2010 and 2030. Married couples' real median incomes will increase by 57 percent between 1990 and 2010 compared with 51 percent for unmarried men and 35 percent for unmarried women. In contrast, married couples' incomes will increase by 50 percent between 2010 and 2030, compared with 55 percent for unmarried men and 59 percent for unmarried women.

Disaggregation of income growth by age group across time helps to explain these patterns (figure 3.1). The projections actually show particularly strong growth in income for all of the "young" elderly--persons age 65 to 69--between 1990 and 2010. Recall that this cohort, born between 1941 and 1945, represents the generation just before the baby boom cohort. As the literature shows, they benefited from the strong economic growth in the U.S. during the 1960s when their careers were beginning and they were well-established by the time the economic difficulties of the post-1973 period began (Michel and Levy 1988).

Table 3.1 PROJECTED REAL MEDIAN INCOME BY
MARITAL STATUS, AGE, AND SEX: 1990-2030
(Baseline assumptions 1988 $)

				Percentage Change	
Group	1990	2010	2030	1990-2010	2010-2030
Married					
couples	$15,500	$24,400	$36,700	+57	+50
65-69	17,300	28,200	40,100	+63	+42
70-79	15,000	23,900	36,800	+60	+54
80+	12,600	16,200	29,100	+28	+80
Unmarried					
men[a]	$7,200	$10,900	$16,900	+51	+55
65-69	8,400	14,700	18,200	+76	+24
70-79	7,600	11,800	17,900	+55	+52
80+	6,300	8,500	14,400	+34	+69
Unmarried					
women	$6,000	$8,100	$12,900	+35	+59
65-69	6,300	10,100	15,000	+59	+48
70-79	6,200	8,400	13,700	+36	+63
80+	5,600	7,300	11,500	+30	+58

Source: The Urban Institute's Dynamic Simulation of Income Model
(DYNASIM).

Notes: The data include the entire elderly population (community-
based plus institutionalized). Income includes Social Security benefits,
private pensions, government pensions, interest and dividend income,
SSI, and earnings.

Numbers rounded to nearest hundred.

a. The unmarried group for men and women includes persons who
were never married and divorced and widowed persons.

Figure 3.1 **Percentage Change in Real Median Income**

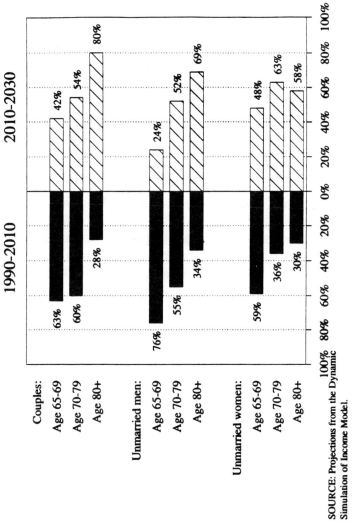

SOURCE: Projections from the Dynamic Simulation of Income Model.

Real incomes for married couples and unmarried men age 70 to 79 also will increase significantly between 1990 and 2010 for similar reasons. Persons in this cohort, many of whom were parents of the baby boom generation, economically outperformed succeeding and preceding cohorts, often by substantial margins. Unmarried women in the same age group did not benefit from the strong economy of the 1960s and 1970s as much as their male counterparts, however. Income for unmarried women age 70 to 79 will increase by 36 percent between 1990 and 2010, compared with 55 percent for unmarried men and 60 percent for couples. This generation of women did not participate in the labor force as fully as their successors and, thus, will not benefit from the favorable economic and pension conditions as much as men will in their retirement years.

The increase in income for the young elderly between 1990 and 2010 will have an enormous impact 20 years later, when this generation reaches their 80s. Real median income for elderly married couples age 80 and older will be 80 percent higher in 2030 than in 2010; income for unmarried men age 80 and older will increase by 69 percent, and income for unmarried women age 80 and older will increase by 58 percent over the same period.

In contrast, the growth in income for the young elderly will be much slower between 2010 and 2030 than that shown for the 1990-2010 period. This cohort, born in the early 1960s, entered the labor force after 1973 during years of sluggish growth or at least of growth rates not as high as the 1960s. Moreover, they will be the first group to experience the *full* effects of the 1983 Social Security Amendments. Under the amendments, the age at which unreduced retirement benefits are available will begin to increase gradually from age 65 in the year 2000 to age 67 in 2022. Benefits for persons retiring before age 67 will be about 12.5 percent lower than they were for preceding cohorts retiring at the same age.[2] As discussed later, the increase in the retirement age is not expected to reduce substantially the proportion of the elderly who retire early. The overwhelming effect of the amendments is likely to be a significant reduction in Social Security benefits.

The 59 percent increase in income shown for unmarried women between 2010 and 2030 is higher than that shown for other family units. This result is explained by increased labor force participation of women and by changes in pension regulations that will increase substantially the proportion of older women who retire with private pensions in the future. For women, these effects offset the reduction in retirement income caused by the 1983 amendments.

The differentials in income growth for elderly men and women in the two periods will affect the future gender gap in income. For example, projected median income for unmarried women is $6,000 in 1990, compared with $7,200 for men (table 3.1)--a difference of 20 percent. But the difference will widen between 1990 and 2010 because of the higher increases in real income for men compared with women discussed above. In 2010, median income for single women will be about 25 percent lower than the income for unmarried men--$8,100 compared with $10,900. The income difference will narrow again after 2010, however, because of the real income gains of elderly women. In 2030 median income for unmarried women will be $12,900, 76 percent of the $16,900 median income shown for men. Moreover, the median income of unmarried women age 65 to 69 will be 82 percent of that shown for men--$15,000 compared with $18,200.

A comparison of these projections with historical patterns shows that the income for the elderly will grow at a somewhat slower pace between 1990 and 2030 than that observed between 1967 and 1984 (table 3.2). The median income of married couples increased by 3.3 percent per year between 1967 and 1984, compared with 2.9 percent during the 1990-2010 period and 2.5 percent between 2010 and 2030. Average increases for unmarried men will be very similar to historic increases. For women, however, there will be a significant decline in the pace of growth between 1990 and 2010 compared with the historic rates shown, but the rapid rate of growth will be restored in the 2010-2030 period. As mentioned earlier, incomes of the elderly during the 1967-84 period were affected by federal policy changes and by a surge in private pension benefits and real interest rates. Similarly, income growth during the 1990-2030 period will be affected by earnings, Social Security policy, accumulation of private and government pension credits, recent policy changes that affect private pensions, and financial asset accumulations. The following section discusses the importance of each source of income for the future elderly.

THE IMPORTANCE OF VARIOUS SOURCES OF INCOME, 1990-2030

The five most important components of income for older Americans--Social Security, private and government pensions, earnings, income from assets, and Supplemental Security Income (SSI)--are included in these projections.[3] The various factors expected to affect these income sources for the future elderly and the assumptions chosen for these projections are discussed below. The retirement age will be a critical factor determining the relative importance of earnings and retirement benefits. Thus, we first discuss the factors that will affect retirement decisions, and why we chose the projection assumptions included in this report. Retirement benefits also will be affected by policy changes already enacted during the 1980s. As mentioned,

Table 3.2   AVERAGE ANNUAL PERCENTAGE CHANGE IN
REAL MEDIAN INCOME: HISTORICAL AND
PROJECTED BY AGE, SEX, AND MARITAL
STATUS

Group	1967-84	1979-84	1990-2010	2010-2030
Married couples	3.3	3.7	2.9	2.5
65-69	--	--	3.2	2.1
70-79	--	--	3.0	2.7
80+	--	--	1.4	4.0
Unmarried men	2.7	2.2	2.5	2.8
65-69	--	--	3.8	1.2
70-79	--	--	2.7	2.6
80+	--	--	1.7	3.5
Unmarried women	3.5	3.0	1.7	3.0
65-69	--	--	3.0	2.4
70-79	--	--	1.8	3.1
80+	--	--	1.5	2.9

Sources: Radner (1987), p. 24, table 19; projections from The Urban
Institute's Dynamic Simulation of Income Model (DYNASIM), baseline
mortality and health assumptions.

Note: For 1967-84 and 1979-84 data, average annual percentage change
in median, pretax income; data not available by age.

the 1983 Social Security Amendments enacted some significant changes in benefits for the 21st century, and the rules
governing private pensions have been changed so that
more elderly persons will have a right to a pension benefit.
Decisions of private companies to have pensions, of
course, will also affect the future of this income source.
The assets component of income, perhaps the most diffi-

cult income source to project, will be affected not only by savings behavior of these cohorts during their working years but by bequests and by the performance of the U.S. economy.

Factors Affecting Retirement Rates

In recent decades, the precipitous decline in the labor force participation of older persons and, hence, the decline in the importance of earnings for the elderly has been significant. Between 1960 and 1986, the labor force participation rates of men and women age 65 and over fell by between 35 and 50 percent (figure 3.2). In 1960, about 43.2 percent of men and 15.8 percent of women age 65 and over had worked sometime during the year, compared with 22.5 and 9.9 percent, respectively, in 1986.

A number of factors--especially the availability of retirement income at younger ages, higher retirement incomes, and the general acceptance of retirement--have encouraged the labor force withdrawal of older workers.[4] Some analysts, however, argue that the future elderly will be enticed to stay in the labor force longer than their predecessors.[5] Recent federal policy changes--the 1983 Social Security Amendments and the elimination of the mandatory retirement age--have been designed to encourage older workers to stay in the labor force. Moreover, additional changes to further influence behavior in this direction, such as the elimination of the Social Security earnings test, are being discussed.

Nevertheless, it appears that the recent pattern of retirement behavior is likely to persist, unless more extreme measures are enacted to influence behavior to the contrary. As discussed below, most of the factors that have contributed to the withdrawal of older workers from the labor force in recent years are expected to continue into the future. Retirement

Figure 3.2   Labor Force Participation Rates of
Workers Age 65 and Over, 1960-86

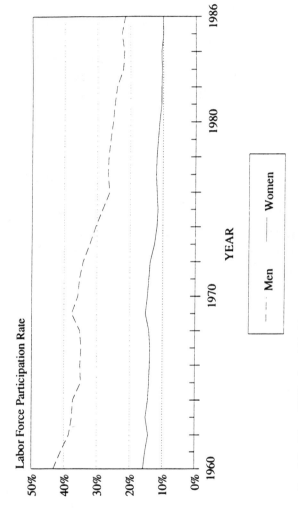

Source: Rosenfeld and Brown (1979) and unpublished data
provided by the U.S. Department of Labor

incomes are expected to increase in real terms, attitudes toward retirement are expected to remain positive, and increases in longevity per se are not expected to increase the retirement age. Increases in female labor force participation at younger ages will not necessarily increase participation at older ages, because more women also will have independent retirement incomes, a factor that will encourage their retirement. Finally, the labor shortage argument becomes weak when future dependency ratios are projected and compared with historic rates.

RETIREMENT INCOME

Increases in retirement benefits over the last several decades have significantly increased the ability of a family to maintain a comfortable standard of living in retirement. As noted earlier, Social Security benefits and private pensions increased dramatically between 1960 and 1984 at the same time that the labor force participation for older persons was rapidly declining. Moreover, this relationship has been confirmed by more than just a casual observation of correlating trends. Various empirical studies have documented that workers respond to the financial incentives built into Social Security and private pension policy.[6]

Future retirement rates will remain influenced by retirement income, and, because retirement incomes are generally expected to continue to increase in real terms, current retirement rates are generally expected to continue into the future. However, there is likely to be a small delay in the retirement age in the 21st century as a result of the 1983 Social Security Amendments. The amendments will raise the age at which full, unreduced Social Security benefits are available beginning in 2000. Benefits will still be available at age 62, but at reduced rates. The bonus for delaying retirement will begin to increase starting in 1990, and the earnings test will increase in 1990 as well. Analysis has suggested that the retirement behavior of of older workers will change only slightly in response to these amendments, however, and this response is incorporated into these projections.[7]

On net, it is likely that private pensions will continue to exert an influence on retirement behavior similar to that observed in recent years. On the one hand, the rapid growth in private pension coverage and benefit levels of the 1960s has slowed in recent years (Kotlikoff and Smith 1983). On the other hand, the percentage of older persons expected to receive pensions in the future will increase during the 1990-2030 period as a result of legislation passed during the 1980s.[8] The effects of changes in pension coverage patterns and legislation governing the rules of private plans are incorporated into these simulations, because they will influence projected private pension benefits and, in turn, the expected retirement age.

ATTITUDES

The positive attitude of workers toward retirement also has influenced the retirement age, and it would be difficult to argue that this attitude will change in the future. As the number of older workers leaving the labor force has increased, so has the acceptability of retirement. When other factors (such as those described above) are also tending to encourage withdrawal from the labor force at older ages, it is difficult to decipher the effects of such subjective factors as the "desire to retire." However, workers more and more frequently cite the "desire to retire" as the main reason for choosing to retire.[9] At the same time, many older workers have expressed a desire to switch from full-time to part-time work. Although a significant percentage of older workers have been able to find part-time work, others have been forced to leave the labor force completely when they could not find part-time work.[10] Thus, the availability of more part-time jobs in the future (particularly, well-paid white-collar jobs) in fact may decrease future labor force withdrawal rates. There is no solid evidence that employers will significantly increase these opportunities in the near future, however.

MORTALITY RATES AND HEALTH

Some argue that decreasing mortality rates *should* encourage workers to delay retirement because a worker may be expected to spend a portion of that additional period in the labor force.[11] However, there has been no evidence of this trend to date. The historical declines in labor force participation of older workers have occurred during a more rapid decline in mortality rates than that included in this study. Thus, this factor is not expected to increase the labor force participation of older persons in these projections.

A source of greater uncertainty perhaps is the future health status of older workers. Because workers with health problems are more likely to leave the labor force than healthy workers, improvements in disability rates could increase the labor force participation rates of the elderly. As discussed in chapter 2, however, it is still not clear whether there will be significant changes in the disability rates of the elderly. Consistent with the baseline scenario, which assumes that recent disability rates will persist, health is not expected to exert an independent effect on the retirement age in these projections.

STRONGER LABOR FORCE ATTACHMENT OF WOMEN

It is also unclear whether recent increases in the labor force participation rates of nonelderly women will increase the percentage of older women in the labor force in the 21st century. On the one hand, as more women with significant labor force experience enter the ranks of the elderly in the 21st century, their rates of participation could look more like those of men. On the other hand, the increased retirement benefits that will result from women's longer work careers will have the opposite effect. These competing effects are incorporated in these projections, because the amount of lifetime labor force experience and potential retirement benefits both affect retirement decisions.

LABOR SHORTAGES

Finally, some analysts argue that the demand for older workers will increase in the 21st century because demographic trends will create a scarcity of workers, and demand will lead to a number of changes that will make work attractive for more older persons.

This argument, however, may be overstated because increases in worker productivity could reduce the required ratio of workers to capital. In addition, even if labor scarcity does occur, some of the problem could be solved by immigration policy. The need for highly trained workers could still remain, however, and that might encourage some employers to adopt policies that would retain more older workers. More importantly, using projections of the ratio of workers to nonworkers, under the assumption that current behavior will persist, we argue that there may be little credence to the labor scarcity argument.

The ratio of the population *not* of working age (either below age 16 or above age 64) is the most commonly used definition of the dependency ratio. Using this definition, the DYNASIM projections, assuming that current retirement rates will essentially persist, show the total dependency ratio steeply increasing from 0.56 to 0.70 between 1990 and 2030 (table 3.3). Most of the increase occurs between 2010 and 2030, when the baby boom generation retires. Notice, however, that the historical comparisons show that the dependency ratio in 2030 will essentially return to the ratio of the 1960s and 1970s.

Moreover, if dependency is measured as the relative size of the population of nonworkers (of any age) to workers, the increase in the dependency ratio between 1990 and 2030 will be smaller--from 0.85 in 1990 to 0.92 in 2030 (table 3.3). In other words, in the year 2030 there will be roughly one nonworker for every working person. Although this ratio will be higher in 2030 than in 1990, this measure of dependency will be considerably lower than the ratios observed before the 1980s. Considering that the U.S. economy was quite strong during the 1960s and 1970s, it is difficult to argue that there will definitely be a significant increase in demand for older workers in the 21st century.[12] An equally plausible argument is that there will be strong incentives for employers to increase worker productivity and, consequently, the economic return to workers, returning to the high levels observed during the 1960s and early 1970s.

Projections of Older Workers and their Earnings, 1990-2030

Because it is difficult to justify a significant change in the labor force behavior of older persons, these projections use the recent behavior of older workers to forecast the future. The Urban Institute's Dynamic Simulation of Income Model (DYNASIM) captures the influence of a number of socioeconomic characteristics (health status, age, sex, wage rate, marital status, pension and Social Security eligibility, and pension and Social Security wealth) on retirement, and changes in these variables will influence future retirement decisions.[13] However, the *marginal* response of retirement to these factors will not change.

Table 3.3   DEPENDENCY RATIOS, USING ALTERNATIVE
DEFINITIONS, BY DECADE, 1960-2030

Definition	1960	1970	1980	1990	2010	2030
Total age dependency ratio[a]	0.72	0.67	0.55	0.56	0.55	0.70
Ratio of nonworkers to workers[b]	1.26	1.14	0.94	0.85	0.78	0.92

Sources: Historical data: *Statistical Abstract of the United States: 1988*, Table 13; Rosenfeld and Brown (1979), and unpublished data provided by the U.S. Department of Labor. 1990-2030 Projections: DYNASIM.

a. The total age dependency ratio is defined as the ratio of (1) the population age 65 and over plus the population under age 16, to (2) the population between age 16 and age 64.

b. The ratio of nonworkers to workers is the ratio of all nonworkers in the population to all workers in the population, no matter the age of the workers and nonworkers.

As shown in table 3.4 the number of older workers will almost double by 2030, from 4.9 to 9.6 million, in the base-case projections. This increase, however, simply reflects the increase in the elderly population--the rate of participation in the labor force will essentially remain constant at about 15 percent between 1990 and 2030. Table 3.4 also shows that there are no significant changes expected in participation by age or sex. These projections indicate that the endogenous variables affecting labor supply (such as the reduction in Social Security benefits or stronger career attachments of many women) will not significantly affect labor force participation rates.

Table 3.4 PROJECTIONS OF WORKERS AND LABOR
FORCE PARTICIPATION RATES, BY AGE AND
SEX: 1990-2030

Group	Millions of Workers			Labor Force Participation Rates		
	1990	2010	2030	1990	2010	2030
Men						
65-69	1.5	1.9	2.9	.33	.34	.34
70-74	0.8	0.8	1.8	.23	.23	.24
75+	0.7	1.0	1.5	.14	.15	.14
Total	3.0	3.8	6.1	.23	.24	.24
Women						
65-69	1.1	1.4	1.8	.19	.21	.19
70-74	0.5	0.6	1.1	.10	.12	.12
75+	0.3	0.3	0.5	.04	.02	.02
Total	1.9	2.3	3.4	.10	.09	.09
Total						
65-69	2.6	3.3	4.7	.25	.26	.26
70-74	1.3	1.5	2.9	.15	.17	.17
75+	1.0	1.3	2.0	.08	.07	.07
Total	4.9	6.1	9.6	.15	.15	.15

Source: Projections from The Urban Institute's Dynamic Simulation of
Income Model (DYNASIM), baseline mortality and health assumptions.

Note: A person is classified as a worker if he or she worked at all
during the year. Labor force participation rates are calculated as the
ratio of total workers to total population by age and sex. See table 2.3
for population totals by age and sex.

Table 3.5   FAMILIES AGE 65 AND OVER WITH EARNINGS,
BY AGE AND MARITAL STATUS: 1990-2030

Age Group	Percentage with Earnings			Average Earnings (1988 dollars)		
	1990	2010	2030	1990	2010	2030
Couples						
65-69	54	56	58	10,300	15,800	21,300
70-79	38	40	41	5,400	7,500	13,600
80+	28	25	24	2,500	3,500	5,700
Total	43	44	45	7,200	10,400	15,100
Unmarried men						
65-69	28	25	25	4,700	7,900	7,100
70-79	14	14	17	1,600	2,200	3,100
80+	6	10	8	600	1,300	1,200
Total	15	15	16	2,000	3,100	3,500
Unmarried women						
65-69	22	23	21	1,600	2,500	3,100
70-79	8	8	8	700	800	1,300
80+	2	0	1	80	40	100
Total	9	8	7	700	800	1,200
Total						
65-69	37	39	39	6,000	9,500	12,100
70-79	19	20	20	2,400	3,300	5,600
80+	6	6	6	500	800	1,200
Total	21	20	20	2,900	4,100	5,800

Source: Projections from The Urban Institute's Dynamic Simulation of
Income Model (DYNASIM), baseline mortality and health assumptions.

Note: Numbers rounded to nearest hundred.

The DYNASIM model, which projects earnings for elderly families, also simulates wage rates and hours worked for older workers who remain in the labor force.[14] Because the elderly are not expected to increase their labor force participation significantly in the 21st century, the percentage of elderly families with earnings will remain essentially unchanged--at roughly 20 percent in the 1990-2030 period (table 3.5). The level of real earnings, however, will double during the 1990-2030 period because of increases in the wage rate. The average level of earnings received by all elderly families will increase from $2,900 in 1990 to $5,800 in 2030.

Increases in real earnings will differ among the various family types shown, with couples having significantly greater increases in this source of income. The projections show couples' earnings increasing by 110 percent--from $7,200 in 1990 to $15,100 in 2030; earnings for single men increasing by 75 percent--from $2,000 to $3,500; and earnings for women increasing by 71 percent--from $700 to $1,200. Earnings for couples are increasing faster than those for unmarried persons because there will be more two-earner couples in 2030.[15]

Retirement Benefits: How Will Current Policies Affect Future Benefits?

A number of policies have been enacted during recent years that will significantly affect Social Security and pension benefits for future cohorts of elderly Americans. These new policies will affect the number of families with income from these sources and the amount of retirement income going to various subgroups of the elderly population, independent of trends in the retirement age and earnings of these cohorts.

In these projections, individual earnings histories are simulated and used to calculate retirement benefits according to the rules expected to be in effect when these persons retire. Simulated earnings histories are a combination of observed earnings and projected earnings thereafter.[16] Average real wage growth and other economic variables such as GNP growth and interest rates are controlled to match the middle-of-the-road assumptions in the 1986 Trustees Report, but individual wage growth may vary from this average, depending on a person's labor force history, education, and so on.[17] Each individual's earnings history is used to calculate benefits that will be payable in their year of retirement. Dependents' and survivors' benefits are also calculated using the appropriate earnings histories of each family member.[18]

SOCIAL SECURITY

As mentioned earlier, several changes in the Social Security system will be important during the projection period as a result of the 1983 Social Security Amendments.[19] The most significant change is the increase in the age at which "full" retirement benefits are payable from age 65 to age 67. This change will occur gradually. Beginning in 2000 and continuing until 2022, the retirement age will increase by two months each year. The increase in the retirement age means that persons who choose to retire before this age still will be able to do so, but their benefits will be reduced. For example, in 2022 someone retiring at age 62 will receive 70 percent of the full benefit payable at age 67, whereas the benefit payable at this age just before 2000 was 80 percent. The 1983 amendments also increased the bonus for those who delay retirement beyond the normal retirement age. Beginning in 1990 the delayed retirement credit will increase gradually from 3 percent to 8 percent per year by 2009. Another factor important to these projections is that more workers will be covered by Social

Security. Beginning in 1984 new federal employees and most political appointees and elected officials were covered.[20]

As illustrated in table 3.6, by 2030 most elderly persons will receive some income from Social Security. Recipiency rates for persons age 65 to 69 will be somewhat lower than for other age groups simply because some have not retired yet. However, after age 70 virtually all elderly families will have some income from Social Security. This represents a change from the earlier period, when some elderly persons were not covered by Social Security. For example, 85 percent of unmarried women in 1990 will have income from Social Security, compared with 96 percent in 2030.

The change in real Social Security benefits mirrors the earlier discussion of the change in real income for elderly families over time, and it also reflects the effects of the 1983 amendments. For example, benefits will be 55 percent higher for married couples age 65 to 69 in 2010 compared with 1990, but benefits for the cohort that succeeds them will increase by just 26 percent over the next 20-year period. Two factors are responsible. One is the "golden age" phenomenon discussed earlier. The older brothers and sisters of the baby boom cohort enjoyed the benefits of a booming economy in the 1960s. The rapid growth in their earnings histories eventually will be reflected in their Social Security benefits. The other factor is that the youngest age cohort shown in 2030 will be the first cohort to experience the full effects of the 1983 amendments. The DYNASIM model projects only a small labor supply response and, therefore, a significant reduction in Social Security benefits as a result of the amendments.

This pattern is not as pronounced for unmarried women. Social Security benefits will increase by 41 percent between 2010 and 2030, compared with 47 percent between 1990 and 2010. As discussed earlier, the cohort of women who will retire in 2030 will have more years in the

Table 3.6 SOCIAL SECURITY BENEFITS: 1990-2030

Social Security Group	Percentage with Income			Average Benefits (1988 $)[a]			Percent Change	
	1990	2010	2030	1990	2010	2030	1990-2010	2010-2030
Married couples	93	96	96	9,200	13,300	18,100	+44	+36
65-69	89	92	91	8,000	12,400	15,600	+55	+26
70-79	95	99	99	10,900	14,700	20,100	+35	+36
80+	99	100	100	10,200	11,800	18,400	+15	+56
Unmarried men	87	91	94	5,600	7,600	10,900	+34	+44
65-69	80	81	87	4,900	7,300	9,800	+50	+33
70-79	85	96	97	6,000	8,600	11,700	+43	+35
80+	93	93	96	5,700	6,700	10,700	+19	+60
Unmarried women	85	93	96	4,800	6,700	10,000	+38	+50
65-69	82	89	92	4,600	6,700	9,500	+47	+41
70-79	83	96	97	5,100	7,000	10,300	+38	+46
80+	89	92	98	4,700	6,200	10,000	+32	+60

Source: Projections of The Urban Institute's Dynamic Simulation of Income Model (DYNASIM), baseline mortality and health assumptions.

Note: Numbers rounded to nearest hundred.

a. Includes units with zero income from source.

labor force than earlier cohorts of women, and, consequently, their Social Security benefits will be higher. This
offsets the reductions in Social Security benefits caused by
the increase in the retirement age.

PENSIONS

Pension benefits from employer- and union-sponsored
plans are an important and growing source of income for
retirees. Elderly families with income from pensions to
supplement their Social Security benefits generally enjoy a
higher standard of living than other elderly families
without this income source.

Several factors will increase the importance of this
income source for older Americans. First, between the
1950s and the 1970s the percentage of the work force
covered by a private pension plan more than doubled.
Between 1950 and 1979, the percentage of private sector
wage and salary workers covered by a pension plan
increased from 25 percent to about 56 percent (Kotlikoff
and Smith 1983). Coverage rates for government workers
increased from 60 to 90 percent during the same period.
Although pension coverage rates took a downturn after
1979, declining to 52 percent of the work force in 1983, the
number of private pension plans and the number of active
participants continued to grow.[21] Between 1979 and 1982
total private corporate and multiemployer plans increased
from 589,000 to 729,000, and the number of active participants increased from 46.9 million to 53.2 million (Beller
1986, p. 80). Essentially, the number of employees covered
and the number of plans covering the work force continue
to grow, whereas proportions of covered workers have
remained fairly stable. Nonetheless, more workers retiring
in the 21st century will have spent the majority of their

careers in covered employment than at any other time in the past.

Second, rules governing private pension plans changed significantly with the passage of the Employee Retirement and Income Security Act (ERISA) in 1974, the Retirement Equity Act in 1984, and the Tax Act of 1986.[22] Between 1942 and 1974 no legislative changes were made in the requirements pension plans had to meet to be ruled a "qualified plan." The long period of legislative inactivity came to an end when ERISA was passed in 1974. ERISA tried to preserve the private system's successes but at the same time to extend coverage and benefits to more workers (Carter 1984). ERISA mandated (prospectively) uniform requirements for coverage and vesting, strengthened and protected pension trust funds, and enacted a series of limitations on plan contributions so that highly compensated employees could no longer be favored over lower-paid employees. The effects of ERISA will be most evident in the 21st century, when retiring workers will have been protected under the ERISA provisions during most of their working careers. The Retirement Equity Act (REA) strengthened protection for survivors of workers with pensions, and it decreased the minimum participation age from 25 to 21. The Tax Act of 1986 enacted 5-year vesting for most private pension plans, in lieu of ERISA's 10-year requirement, and the integration limits were changed so that more low-wage workers will receive an adequate pension in the future. Because both of these laws also apply to prospective accrual of benefits, their full effects will be observed for workers retiring in the 21st century.

The third factor that will increase pension recipiency in the future is the fact that women, on average, will have spent more years in the labor force than their predecessors. Thus, they will be more likely to have pension income when they retire.

Pensions will be much more common in the future (table 3.7). In fact, the vast majority of elderly families will have some pension income. The increases in pension recipiency will be greatest for unmarried women. In 1990 only about one-quarter of unmarried women are expected to have some income from a pension, compared with about three-quarters in 2030.

These projections show that pension income will continue to vary significantly by sex, marital status, and age. Pensions will continue to decline with age because recipiency rates will be somewhat lower for the older age groups, because pensions will reflect real earnings before retirement and each age cohort's earnings will generally be higher in real terms, and because pensions are not expected to be fully indexed during retirement.[23] It is also shown that although many more women are expected to have pensions in the future, their pensions will be much lower than those for men. On average, pension benefits for single men in 2030 are more than double pension benefits for single women ($6,300 compared with $2,930). But the difference between the pension benefits of men and women in the youngest age category indicates a considerable narrowing of this gap in the future. Benefits for unmarried men age 65 to 69 will be $6,300 compared with $4,100 for unmarried women age 65 to 69, a difference of 54 percent. The relatively high lifetime work experience of this cohort of women will significantly increase their retirement benefits.

Asset Income: A Real Unknown?

Asset income is also important to elderly families, particularly as a source of income that augments retirement benefits. These projections focus on the financial assets of elderly families--that is, assets that typically earn a "rate of

Table 3.7 PENSION BENEFITS: 1990-2030

Group	Percentage with Income			Average Pension[a]			Percent Change	
	1990	2010	2030	1990	2010	2030	1990-2010	2010-2030
Married couples	60	86	93	2,330	6,310	10,550	+170	+67
65-69	59	86	90	2,800	7,280	11,240	+160	+54
70-79	63	87	95	2,290	6240	10,750	+172	+72
80+	48	82	94	640	3,710	8,810	+480	+137
Unmarried men	43	70	85	1,380	3,980	6,300	+188	+58
65-69	51	74	82	1,950	5,250	6,300	+169	+20
70-79	48	75	86	1,710	3,760	7,040	+120	+87
80+	31	61	84	540	2,490	5,370	+360	+116
Unmarried women	26	50	73	470	1,210	2,930	+157	+142
65-69	35	63	77	700	2,230	4,100	+219	+84
70-79	30	57	79	620	1,380	3,470	+123	+151
80+	15	37	65	140	600	1,840	+329	+207

Source: Projections of The Urban Institute's Dynamic Simulation of Income Model (DYNASIM), baseline mortality and health assumptions.

Note: Figures include private, federal, and state and local pensions.

a. Includes units with zero income from source.

return" and pay a stream of income to their owner. Included are savings accounts, checking accounts, stocks, bonds, and trusts.[24] Because DYNASIM does not include an "asset accumulation" model, current asset distributions are used to infer the future distribution of assets.[25] But as we discuss below, there are many uncertainties regarding the level and distribution of financial assets among the future elderly. These projections preserve only one possible scenario. Basically we assume that, on average, real growth in financial assets will track real growth in GNP, and that income from assets will match the expected rate-of-return on U.S. Treasury notes. The model, however, distributes asset holdings among families according to their individual socioeconomic characteristics.

METHODS OF ESTIMATING ASSET INCOME

The estimates start with a prediction of the stock of assets held by elderly families as shown in the Survey of Consumer Finances (SCF). In 1983, these data showed that almost 80 percent of elderly families held some financial assets (table 3.8), but relatively few had substantial assets. Only 7 percent of elderly families held $100,000 or more in financial assets in 1983, whereas more than 50 percent of elderly families held less than $5,000 in financial assets.[26] A distribution of assets is imputed to elderly families in the future based on a model that captures the relationships between assets and socioeconomic characteristics in these data. The model uses an estimation technique that accounts for the fact that the distribution of assets is heavily skewed, and families cannot have a negative value of financial assets.[27] The important variables found to affect holdings of financial assets are age, race, marital status, education level, disability, home ownership, and income from Social Security, pensions, and earnings. Assets are

Table 3.8 DISTRIBUTION OF TOTAL FINAN-
CIAL ASSETS IN 1983: PERCENT-
AGE OF THE POPULATION AGE 65
AND OVER

Income Level	Percentage of Total Population
None	21.1
$1 to $499	11.2
$500 to $999	7.0
$1,000 to $4,999	17.2
$5,000 to $9,999	9.1
$10,000 to $24,999	13.0
$25,000 to $49,999	8.0
$50,000 to $99,999	6.6
$100,000 and over	6.9

Source: 1983 Survey of Consumer Finances.

inversely related to age, for example, and females and
blacks have lower assets than others. The positive correlates include other retirement income, education, home
ownership, and marriage.

Whereas these relationships are used to impute a distribution of assets, several important assumptions are made
about the growth of asset income for the future elderly.
First, asset levels are assumed to be related to a family's
relative income position, not to their absolute income
level.[28] Correspondingly, the projections of future assets
are based on the relative income position of future elderly

families. Real asset levels are highly correlated with other income. If real growth in other income sources were used to predict the real level of future assets, the growth in asset income would be overstated. That is, the future elderly will have higher real levels of Social Security and pension benefits than their predecessors, reflecting the lifetime earnings growth of each successive cohort, but this does not mean that they will be as well-off as elderly persons with the same income in 1983 (adjusted for prices). This methodology means that real assets will not grow with real levels of retirement income. Instead, a straightforward assumption was made that real growth in assets would follow the real growth in GNP between 1983 and the year of the projection, based on the middle-of-the-road economic assumptions of the 1986 Social Security Trustees Report.

Of course, the caveat associated with these projections is that the relationships observed between characteristics of the elderly in the 1980s may not be good predictors of these associations in the future. For example, if the future elderly who are very old have to spend down more (or less) of their assets on health care, then these projections will overstate (or understate) future asset holdings for this age group. In addition, some may argue that the assumption that assets will grow with real growth in GNP will overstate assets for this cohort. Many observers have noted that the savings rate of recent generations, particularly the baby boom generation, has lagged behind the savings rate of their parents (Michel and Levy 1988; Greenwood and Wolff 1988). If workers continue to save at a low rate, then these projections may overstate asset accumulations. However, others increasingly argue that this has been a life-cycle effect and that savings rates will increase in the future as the baby boom generation matures. In addition, baby boomers are likely to inherit substantial wealth from their parents.

The final important assumption underlying the projections of income from assets presented here is the assumed rate of return earned by elderly families on their holdings of financial assets. The interest rate assumption used to derive the projections is the middle-of-the-road interest rate assumption included in the 1986 Social Security Trustees Report--6.4 percent in 1990 and 6.1 percent in 2010 and 2030.

Almost all elderly families will receive some income from assets in the future according to the baseline mortality and disability projections (table 3.9). Moreover, recipiency rates will be fairly constant over the 1990-2030 period. Recipiency rates will be somewhat lower for unmarried persons than for married couples and for very old compared with younger elderly families.

These projections of asset income, of course, will be heavily influenced by the rate of growth in GNP. Between 1990 and 2010 real GNP is expected to grow by 55 percent, and between 2010 and 2030 real GNP will grow by 46 percent. The projections, however, also will be affected by the changing composition of the elderly population. For example, as the population becomes older between 1990 and 2010 this will dampen the growth in assets relative to GNP. Because relatively more elderly will have health limitations, this, too, will dampen the growth in assets.

The projections indicate that the percentage increase in median asset income for married couples will be somewhat less than the increase in GNP (table 3.9). In part, this result reflects the changing demographics of married couples. Relatively more elderly couples will be in the 85-and-older category over time, for example, and this will dampen average real growth in assets for the entire married group, because assets decline with age. Note, however, that the growth in asset income for the 80-and-older married group between 1990 and 2010 exceeds the growth in GNP, because other socioeconomic changes in

Table 3.9 INCOME FROM FINANCIAL ASSETS FOR ALL ELDERLY FAMILIES

Group	Percentage with Income			Median Income (1988 $)[a]			Percentage Change	
	1990	2010	2030	1990	2010	2030	1990-2010	2010-2030
Married couples	96	97	96	580	830	1,100	+43	+34
65-69	95	96	95	560	800	1,040	+43	+30
70-79	97	97	97	630	960	1,270	+52	+32
80+	95	95	94	430	700	870	+63	+24
Unmarried men	86	88	87	80	120	180	+55	+51
65-69	89	91	86	90	150	210	+67	+40
70-79	88	90	89	100	180	250	+80	+39
80+	83	84	84	40	70	100	+75	+43
Unmarried women	89	88	87	80	100	160	+35	+56
65-69	90	88	88	110	140	200	+27	+44
70-79	91	89	88	110	170	240	+52	+41
80+	86	87	86	30	50	80	+69	+60

Source: Projections of The Urban Institute's Dynamic Simulation of Income Model (DYNASIM), baseline mortality and health assumptions.

Note: The table includes all elderly families age 65 and older (whether or not they have asset income). It also includes income from savings, stocks, bonds, and trusts.

a. Dollars rounded to nearest tens.

this subgroup will improve the asset picture for them (for example, more will have private pensions, a positive correlate with financial assets).

Asset income for unmarried elderly persons generally will improve more than that shown for married couples. However, their median asset income still will be relatively low. For example, the median for unmarried men will be $180 in 2030, implying financial asset holdings of $2,920 (in 1988 dollars), and the median for unmarried women in 2030 will be $160, implying $2,660 in financial assets.

Thus, on the whole, these are relatively conservative projections of asset income. As shown earlier, the share of income provided by financial assets will decline in importance for elderly families, especially between 2010 and 2030. Relatively few elderly families will have substantial financial assets, maintaining a distribution similar to that observed in 1983.

Relative Shares of Aggregate Income

Because of the changes in each source of income discussed above, the relative importance of each income source will vary in importance across family units and across the 1990-2030 period (table 3.10). For all elderly families, Social Security benefits will remain the most important income source. But Social Security will decline in importance across time, and the pension component of income becomes more important. Earnings will rank second in importance (on an average basis) for married couples through 2030, and for unmarried men through 1990, but for unmarried women earnings will be less important. Some of these differences reflect different demographic and economic characteristics of each family unit. Married couples, for example, include families with younger spouses who still may have substantial earnings.

Table 3.10   SHARES OF AGGREGATE INCOME: PROJEC-
TIONS FOR ELDERLY COUPLES AND
UNMARRIED PERSONS (1988 $)

	1990	2010	2030
Married Couples			
Thousands of couples	(8,013)	(10,089)	(15,443)
Mean income	$21,700	$38,800	$49,600
Median income	$15,500	$24,400	$36,700
Percentage of income from:			
Social Security	42	37	37
Pensions	11	18	21
Earnings	33	28	30
Assets	14	16	11
Other	--	1	1
Total	100	100	100
Unmarried Men			
Thousands of persons	(4,576)	(5,895)	(10,272)
Mean income	$9,900	$15,600	$21,600
Median income	$7,200	$10,900	$16,900
Percentage of income from:			
Social Security	57	48	49
Pensions	14	23	29
Earnings	20	20	16
Assets	6	8	4
Other	3	1	2
Total	100	100	100

	1990	2010	2030
	Unmarried Women		
Thousands of persons	(13,407)	(17,314)	(25,346)
Mean income	$6,800	$9,600	$14,600
Median income	$6,000	$8,100	$12,900
Percent of income from:			
Social Security	71	69	68
Pensions	7	13	20
Earnings	10	8	8
Assets	3	7	3
Other	9	3	1
Total	100	100	100

Source: Projections from The Urban Institute's Dynamic Simulation of Income Model (DYNASIM), baseline mortality and health assumptions.

Notes: Includes entire elderly population (community-based plus institutionalized). Pension income includes private, federal, and state and local pensions. Asset income includes interest, dividends, and returns from bonds, estates, and trusts. Projections *exclude* potential income from military pensions, veterans' pensions, unemployment compensation, and workmen's compensation. Other category includes Supplemental Security Income (SSI) benefits.

The unmarried female group includes a substantial number of widows and very elderly persons, many of whom have very low incomes. Finally, income from assets will be more important to married couples than to singles, consistent with the higher income status of this group.

DISTRIBUTIONAL OUTCOMES

Although these projections paint a fairly rosy portrait of the income of the future elderly population, there will still be pockets of the elderly population with low incomes. In 40 years, what we now know as the poverty threshold ($5,670 for a single elderly person in 1988) will be fairly meaningless. Because incomes rise in real terms, and the poverty threshold is only adjusted for price inflation, by definition the proportion of elderly families in poverty will decline over time. Thus, it is more useful to focus on the distribution of income among elderly families (table 3.11) to examine how many elderly will be at risk financially.

These distributions confirm the low income position of unmarried elderly persons relative to married couples.[29] Unmarried women in particular will be at risk financially. Almost 35 percent of unmarried women will have incomes under $5,000 in 1990, for example, compared with 21 percent of the unmarried men. Women will continue to fall into the lowest income categories more frequently than men through 2030.

As would be expected, elderly families tend to move up in the income distribution over time. By 2030, for example, there will be no married couples with incomes below $5,000, and only 1.7 percent of unmarried men and 4 percent of unmarried women will have incomes this low. However, there will be considerable clustering of unmarried women and men in relatively low income categories in 2030. Roughly 60 percent of single women and 40 percent of single men will have incomes below $15,000 in 2030. In contrast, 80 percent of married couples will have incomes that are $25,000 or more.

Table 3.11 DISTRIBUTION OF CASH INCOME FOR
ELDERLY FAMILIES: 1990-2030

Income	1990	2010	2030
	Married Couples		
< $5,000	2.5%	.2%	--
5,000 < 10,000	15.9	2.6	.5
10,000 < 15,000	28.6	12.4	2.0
15,000 < 20,000	20.3	19.1	6.2
20,000 < 25,000	11.8	17.8	10.4
25,000 < 50,000	15.0	36.0	50.0
50,000+	5.8	11.9	30.9
Total families	100.0%	100.0%	100.0%
(in thousands)	8,074	10,091	18,941
	Unmarried Men		
< $5,000	20.9%	7.6%	1.7%
5,000 < 10,000	52.4	36.8	15.8
10,000 < 15,000	16.1	26.8	23.7
15,000 < 20,000	4.4	13.4	19.9
20,000 < 25,000	2.5	6.3	13.8
25,000 < 50,000	2.3	6.3	20.5
50,000+	1.4	2.8	4.6
Total persons	100.0%	100.0%	100.0%
(in thousands)	4,611	5,895	11,369

Income	1990	2010	2030
	Unmarried Women		
< $5,000	34.9%	18.0%	4.0%
5,000 < 10,000	52.8	49.8	27.4
10,000 < 15,000	8.6	22.2	29.5
15,000 < 20,000	1.8	5.4	20.6
20,000 < 25,000	.7	2.1	9.0
25,000 < 50,000	.8	1.6	8.1
50,000+	.4	.9	1.4
Total persons	100.0%	100.0%	100.0%
(in thousands)	13,374	17,315	27,280

Source: Projections of The Urban Institute's Dynamic Simulation of Income Model (DYNASIM), baseline mortality and health assumptions.

Note: Includes all elderly whether in the community or in institutions.

a. Income, in 1988 dollars, is pretax and includes earnings, Social Security benefits, private and government pensions, income from financial assets, and Supplemental Security Income.

Some of the income disparities among different types of elderly families are, of course, caused by differences in demographic composition. Unmarried women tend to be very old, but married couples tend to be relatively young. Income will vary significantly by the age and health status characteristics of elderly persons. Persons in the lowest income quartile, or the bottom one-fourth of the income distribution, will be at greater risk financially than other families.[30] In 2030 there will be 2.607 million unmarried elderly persons age 85 and older in the bottom income quartile (36 percent), and 2.366 million (34 percent) in the second income quartile (table 3.12). Thus, 70 percent of the elderly population most at risk demographically in 2030--those unmarried and very old--will fall into the bottom half of the income distribution.

Similarly, the elderly with extensive health needs will fall disproportionately into the lowest income quartiles.[31] For example, 3.245 million single elderly persons will have two or three ADLs in 2030, and 1.044 million of them (31 percent) will fall into the lowest income quartile (table 3.12). Among the 3.570 million with four or more ADL limitations, 1.120 million (31 percent) will fall into the lowest income quartile.

On a positive note, however, the majority of the elderly in the bottom income quartile will have no serious health limitations. Of a total of 8.9 million unmarried persons in the bottom income quartile, 5.9 million (66 percent) will have no serious health limitations. In contrast, 80 percent of elderly, unmarried persons in the top income quartile have no serious health limitations.

Thus, this chapter presents a mixed picture of the future income status of the elderly. On a relatively positive note, incomes of the elderly are expected to continue to grow in real terms. But, income growth is not expected to match recent historical experience; it will be particularly slower after 2010. Married couples are expected to maintain their relatively high income position. However, the relative income picture will brighten somewhat for unmarried persons. The effects of recent earnings gains for women and increases in pension eligibility will be particularly evident in 2030, and the gap between incomes for elderly unmarried men and women will narrow somewhat by 2030.

Table 3.12   ELDERLY PERSONS BY INCOME QUARTILE,
AGE, AND HEALTH STATUS

	Income Quartile				
	I	II	III	IV	All
1990					
Married couples[a]	($0)	($10,900)	($15,500)	($22,900)	
Persons (000s)	3,500	3,674	3,497	3,318	13,988
By age:					
65-69	1,333	1,487	1,661	1,740	6,221
70-74	1,119	1,135	961	870	4,085
75-79	581	704	637	490	2,412
80-84	297	277	206	158	938
85+	170	71	32	59	332
By ADLs:					
0	2,966	3,263	3,132	2,970	12,331
1	198	194	158	142	692
2-3	218	138	127	115	598
4+	119	79	79	91	368
Unmarried persons[a] ($0)		($4,800)	($6,300)	($8,600)	
Persons (000s)	4,614	4,328	4,489	4,501	17,932
By age:					
65-69	929	831	949	1,416	4,125
70-74	1,020	914	1,020	1,159	4,113
75-79	929	724	965	1,099	3,717
80-84	957	744	728	570	2,999
85+	779	1,115	827	257	2,978
By ADLs:					
0	3,393	2,998	3,275	3,682	13,348
1	392	392	396	348	1,528
2-3	396	431	411	277	1,515
4+	435	506	407	194	1,542

	Income Quartile				
	I	II	III	IV	All
			2010		
Married couples[a]	($2,800)	($17,500)	($24,400)	($35,700)	
Persons (000s)	4,597	4,574	4,364	4,298	17,833
By age:					
65-69	1,186	1,917	2,389	2,303	
70-74	981	1,351	1,215	1,219	4,766
75-79	895	809	493	460	2,656
80-84	862	357	197	189	1,605
85+	673	140	70	127	1,010
By ADLs:					
0	3,768	4,011	3,855	3,871	15,505
1	250	246	263	189	948
2-3	291	156	135	131	714
4+	287	160	111	197	665
Unmarried persons[a]	($0)	($6,100)	($8,600)	($12,100)	
Persons (000s)	5,824	5,826	5,818	5,915	23,382
By age:					
65-69	751	895	1,088	2,196	5,030
70-74	796	887	1,120	1,384	4,187
75-79	1,071	944	1,232	981	4,228
80-84	1,301	1,195	1,129	624	4,249
85+	1,905	1,905	1,248	731	5,788
By ADLs:					
0	3,887	3,875	4,195	4,770	16,728
1	546	595	525	447	2,114
2-3	620	595	517	365	2,098
4+	772	759	579	333	2,442

	Income Quartile				
	I	II	III	IV	All
		2030			
Married couples[a]	($3,200)	($26,600)	($36,700)	($51,800)	
Persons (000s)	7,073	7,128	6,883	6,967	28,051
By age:					
65-69	1,969	2,531	2,919	3,198	10,617
70-74	1,758	2,193	2,049	2,303	8,303
75-79	1,496	1,344	1,086	972	4,898
80-84	1,043	773	630	359	2,805
85+	807	287	199	135	1,428
By ADLs:					
0	5,847	6,177	6,070	6,249	24,380
1	427	494	338	313	2,949
2-3	435	250	228	292	1,205
4+	363	207	245	114	929
Unmarried persons[a]	($0)	($9,400)	($13,800)	($19,200)	
Persons (000s)	8,948	9,025	9,100	9,269	36,342
By age:					
65-69	1,327	1,449	1,935	2,615	7,326
70-74	1,622	1,724	2,049	2,801	8,196
75-79	1,808	1,745	2,053	1,732	7,338
80-84	1,584	1,741	1,669	1,166	6,160
85+	2,607	2,366	1,394	955	7,322
By ADLs:					
0	5,911	6,029	6,980	7,364	26,284
1	870	900	744	731	3,245
2-3	1,044	976	634	592	3,245
4+	1,124	1,120	744	583	3,570

Source: Projections from The Urban Institute's Dynamic Simulation of Income Model (DYNASIM), using baseline mortality and health assumptions.

Note: ADLs refer to number of limitations in activities of daily living.
a. Figures in parentheses represent the lower income bound.

On a less positive note, substantial numbers of elderly persons will remain at risk financially in the future. For example, about 60 percent of unmarried women are expected to have incomes below $15,000 in 2030 (in 1988 dollars), a sum not likely to provide a "comfortable" retirement living in the future. Moreover, financial risk will continue to be greatest during the period when senior citizens are very old, alone, and have limitations in activities of daily living.

Notes, chapter three

1. The real rate of return on assets has increased significantly in recent years. For example, the 60-month U.S. Treasury bill rate was 4.6 percent in 1967, compared with an inflation rate of 3.1 percent; it rose to 10 percent in 1979, when the inflation rate rose to 11.1 percent; and interest rates peaked at 13.8 percent in 1981, when inflation was 10.3 percent. Rates dropped back to 9.8 percent in 1984, but the inflation rate was only 4.3 percent. (Calculated from the change in the consumer price index, the *Economic Report of the President* 1989, and from Radner 1988.)

2. The 1983 amendments also implemented taxation of one-half of benefits for the Social Security beneficiaries with incomes in excess of (nominal dollar) thresholds of $25,000 for singles and $32,000 for couples beginning in 1984. The effects of these reductions become more important over time as the incomes of more of the elderly exceed these thresholds. Because these projections show only pretax income, this reduction in disposable retirement income is not taken into account.

3. Several sources of income that are important to older Americans are not included in these projections--income from military pensions, veterans' pensions, unemployment compensation, workers' compensation, and personal contributions. This is not because they are not considered important but simply because resources were not sufficient to model these income

components. In 1986 the omitted income components provided 11 percent of the income of older Americans. Veterans' benefits accounted for 5 percent of the total omitted income, military pensions for 2 percent, and the remaining omitted income was spread across the other categories (Grad 1988).

4. For a full review of this literature, see Mitchell and Fields (1982) and Danziger, Haveman, and Plotnick (1981).

5. See Quinn and Burkhauser (1988) for a review of these arguments.

6. See, for example, Fields and Mitchell (1984a), Gustman and Steinmeier (1984, 1985), Burkhauser (1979), Clark and Johnson (1980), Boskin (1977), Burtless and Hausman (1980), and Sammartino (1982).

7. For example, Fields and Mitchell (1984b, p. 57) found a very small elasticity with respect to Social Security benefit: on the order of 0.1 or less, and Storey, Michel, and Zedlewski (1984, p. 62) found a 1.5 percent increase in the number of persons age 62 and older working in 2030 as a result of the 1983 amendments. Other analyses that support these findings include Burtless and Moffitt (1984) and Gustman and Steinmeier (1985).

8. As discussed later, various changes have been made to the Employee Retirement Income Security Act that were designed to provide pension benefits to more covered workers. The 1986 Tax Act, for example, reduced the minimum time at which pension benefits must be vested from 10 years to 5 years.

9. For example, 40 percent of persons who recently became new beneficiaries of Social Security cited the "desire to retire" as their reason for retirement (Sherman 1985). In contrast, Stecker (1951) found that only 4 to 6 percent of retirees in the late 1940s reported that they left employment because they "desired retirement."

10. A number of authors have described this phenomenon. See Quinn and Burkhauser (1988) for a discussion of this literature.

11. Sammartino (1982) summarizes the literature dealing with the effects of mortality and health status on the labor force participation of older workers.

12. The only difference between 2030 and 1960 is that in 2030 society will include a large population of older persons, whereas in 1960, the population of nonworkers included a large population of children. To argue that the "burden" in 2030 will be greater than the "burden" in 1960, one has to argue that older persons are a larger burden on society than young persons were in 1960. This is a debatable assumption. See Aaron (1986) for a discussion of this point.

13. For a full description of this model see Johnson and Zedlewski (1989).

14. As described in Johnson and Zedlewski (1989), hours worked is related to age, unearned income, an expected wage rate, health status, marital status, and the presence of children under age 6 in the family. Wage rates are a function of education, geographic region, health, marital status, age, and last year's wage rate. Real wage growth in the DYNASIM model is also adjusted annually for assumed increases in productivity, using the 1986 II-B assumptions of the Social Security Administration (Board of Trustees 1986). Thus, the model distributes wage rates according to a predictive equation, but real wage increases overall are controlled to match the assumption of the Social Security Administration.

15. As mentioned earlier, many couples categorized as "elderly" have younger spouses with substantial earnings. There will be more two-earner couples primarily because of the increased labor force participation of nonelderly women.

16. The DYNASIM model ages a Current Population Survey that has been matched with earnings histories (from 1951 through 1973), and longitudinal family and earnings histories are developed by simulating major demographic and labor market events on a year-by-year basis.

17. See Johnson and Zedlewski (1989) for a full description of this methodology.

18. See Johnson and Zedlewski (1989) for a description of the Social Security benefit model.

19. See Svahn and Ross (1983) for a full description of the 1983 amendments.

20. Some important changes in tax laws, not included in these projections, will also effectively reduce benefits payable to future elderly relative to today. The 1983 amendments introduced taxation of 50 percent of Social Security benefits for elderly persons with adjusted gross incomes above $25,000 if single, or $32,000 if married. Because these thresholds are fixed, an increasing proportion of elderly families will be paying taxes on their benefits in the future. See Storey, Michel, and Zedlewski (1984).

21. Andrews (1985) reported that the percent of the work force covered by a pension plan declined from 56 percent in May 1979 to 52 percent in May 1983. Her estimates were based on an analysis of the May 1979 and the May 1983 Pension Supplements to the Current Population Survey.

22. The 1982 Tax Equity and Fiscal Responsibility Act (TEFRA), represented a significant change in the favorable tax treatment of pensions, but these changes will not directly affect the projections shown here. See Carter (1984) and The Congressional Budget Office (1987).

23. These projections assume that the historic average adjustment in pensions--about one-half the CPI--will continue into the future as reported in Ippolito and Kolodrubetz (1986). But federal pensions will be fully indexed with inflation.

24. These projections emphasize financial assets because they generally produce an income stream that is used by the elderly to support consumption and are always included in measures of their cash income. Home equity, another important financial

asset, is not included in the projections. We do show projections of the number of future elderly who are likely to own their own home in chapter 6. Estimation of the amount of home equity for owners was beyond the scope of the project.

25. A model that simulates asset accumulations year by year according to knowledge about individual savings behavior would have intuitive appeal and would be more in the spirit of the simulation modules that project other income sources. However, this type of model is difficult to estimate. There is considerable disagreement about factors that influence savings behavior, and in particular, how savings behavior changes over the life cycle. See Lesnoy and Leimer (1985), for example, for a review of this literature.

26. Data from the Survey of Income and Program Participation also confirm this distribution. See Radner (1989).

27. See McBride and Hacker (1989) for a full description of this model.

28. That is, the predictive variables for the other income sources were divided by the median income for these variables for all families in the same age and marital status category before the assets model was estimated.

29. These distributions cannot be compared exactly with similar distributions from recent CPS files because, as noted earlier, some income is not simulated. The important comparisons are the change in income over time and among different types of elderly families.

30. Income quartiles, calculated separately for married couples and unmarried persons, divide the population into four relatively equal groups according to their level of cash income.

31. Although it is true that the projections of income do not *directly* depend on health status, a number of variables that affect incomes also affect the health status outcomes. Examples include age, sex, marital status, and race. These indirect link-

ages, however, are not strong enough to capture the effect of health expenditures on income. Thus, they should be interpreted with caution.

Chapter Four

MEETING THE LONG-TERM CARE
NEEDS OF THE ELDERLY

The changing profile of the elderly population will dramatically affect the long-term care needs of the elderly population.[1] Long-term care (LTC) refers to health, social, and residential services provided to chronically disabled persons over an extended period. The need for long-term care arises from physical or mental disabilities that impair functioning in activities necessary for daily living, conditions often associated with age. In fact, elderly persons are the primary recipients of long-term care services, although many nonaged people also require such care.

Projections presented in this report show that the number of elderly with limitations in activities of daily living (ADLs) will more than double over the next 40 years, if current disability rates persist. This trend alone will certainly increase the need for long-term care services. But the absolute demand for formal long-term care services (both in the home and in institutions) is uncertain. Demand also will be sensitive to the future availability of family care givers and to the elderly's ability to purchase these services. Moreover, this chapter illustrates that a variety of public policies could potentially restrain the increasing demand for long-term care services, particularly the demand for services provided in institutional settings.

In fact, this chapter suggests that there will be a tremendous need for home-care services and paid care givers to replace some of the care now being provided by family members. A much higher proportion of the elderly will be living alone, and relatively few will have children who can provide care for them at home. But this chapter also illustrates that many of the elderly will be able to pay for some of these services in the future because of the expected real gains in income, especially for the frail elderly beginning in 2010. A policy that encourages the elderly who can afford to do so to purchase long-term care insurance when they are young and still healthy and one that encourages the development of private insurance policies that cover not only nursing home care, but in-home care services as well, will be especially important. Despite the real growth in income that is expected, not many will be able to afford to pay for nursing home care out-of-pocket. The chapter also emphasizes that a policy will be needed to help the low-income elderly pay for these services.

Thus, the premise of this chapter is that although some factors driving the need for care are "inevitable," many are within our power to influence. First, some disability may be averted through policies on medical research and a heightened emphasis on improved lifestyles and accident prevention. Second, the health care delivery system could be reformed so that coordinated social and medical services are provided at key junctures to limit the need for long-term care or to provide it in a home or community rather than an institutional setting. Third, a variety of financing reforms hold the potential to spread the burden of paying for long-term care equitably across the population. Indeed, the most promising reforms will weave together reforms in the delivery and financing of long-term care.

Thus, the four most important social policy goals for long-term care should be the *prevention* of disability to the extent possible, the *encouragement and facilitation* of independent living among those who have chronic disability, *efficient delivery* of long-term care services, and *development* of financing mechanisms to make long-term care *affordable* for all older Americans.

As shown below, the current mix of public and private long-term care policies is not well suited to meet these basic goals, and it will be even less well suited to do so in the future. There is a heavy emphasis on maintenance and on dealing with the effects of disability, to the neglect of prevention. Reimbursement policies remain institutionally biased, in the face of clear preferences among people with limitations on their daily living for care received in non-institutional settings. The long-term care system is fragmented and poorly coordinated with acute care, leading to inefficiency in the delivery of care. And there is too much reliance on out-of-pocket outlays that become unaffordable for many Americans after short periods of chronic illness.

Thus, the main purpose of this chapter is to assess a variety of public and private sector policies that will change this system to serve the needs of the future elderly population. The analysis presents a menu of ways to adjust to the changing needs of the elderly population, ranging from the prevention of disability to changes in the way long-term care is organized and delivered, along with innovations in financing. The analysis will highlight areas in which current long-term care policy is not well matched with objective reality and with the changing needs of our senior citizens. It will illustrate the nature and dimensions of the mismatches between social policy and social needs. Finally, the chapter will outline a policy agenda to reduce the observed or predicted mismatches.

HOW DOES THE CURRENT SYSTEM WORK?

The current system of providing long-term care is heavily dominated by two types of care. First, people receive care at home for as long as they can, and most of this care is provided by a family member. Indeed, about 72 percent of all long-term care for the elderly is provided by a family member (Doty, Liu, and Wiener 1985). Second, people enter nursing homes, where long-term care is really a mixture of health services, housing, and other services in an institutional living arrangement.

This dichotomy, of course, is an oversimplification. Some people living at home receive services associated with the term "home care," such as visiting nurses, adult day care, or physical therapy. And there are new forms of congregate living, such as life care communities, that offer alternatives to a nursing home for people who no longer can live alone, or who do not wish to live alone. Nonetheless, as shown in the next chapter, these home care services are quite limited, and the new forms of noninstitutional congregate living at this point serve only a relatively small number of people.

Some basic facts illustrate the relative order of importance of these living arrangements under the current system. In 1982 an estimated 1.4 million elderly persons were in a nursing home on any given day (Doty, Liu, and Wiener 1985, p. 70). But another 1.6 million disabled elderly received help from their spouse; 1.7 million disabled elderly received help from their offspring; 1.4 million received care from a relative other than spouse or child; and only 0.8 million received paid care in their homes. Thus, the bulk of long-term care services are provided informally by family members.

Beyond the numbers, the reality is that most people who require assistance with daily living are cared for at home by a family member until either the deteriorating condition of the patient or the exhaustion of the family member necessitate entry into a nursing home. For most people, there is not much in between. As explained below, the current payment system heavily influences the pattern of use that often translates into a nursing-home-or-nothing choice.

HOW DOES FINANCING OPERATE?

An important factor that leads to this "all or nothing" situation is the way that long-term care is financed. Basically, the payment system is this: A family pays out-of-pocket until it is broke, and then the person qualifies for welfare-based Medicaid assistance. This assistance is tied not only to impoverishment but also to receiving care in a nursing home. Thus, there are really two problems: (1) that long-term care is financed through a combination of household payments and welfare instead of through an insurance model that spreads the risk across a broad base of the population; and (2) that financing is tied to institutional care, even though most people would prefer to receive care at home, wherever possible. The public policy message is that society pays for paupers in nursing homes, and it pays very little otherwise, with the exception of scattered and limited outlays for home care. The victims of disability--and their families--pay the rest themselves.

Expenditures for long-term care services clearly illustrate this situation. Of the $40.6 billion spent for nursing home care in the United States in 1987, only $600 million, or 1.4 percent, was paid for through Medicare, and only $400 million, or 0.9 percent, was financed by private health insurance. Thus, only 2.3 percent of the total nursing home bill in 1987 was financed through an insurance system--public or private. Direct patient payments accounted for $20.0 billion, or 49 percent of the total amount spent, whereas Medicaid, a means-tested public assistance program, paid for $17.8 billion, or 44 percent. The remaining 5 percent of the expenditures were paid for through other government programs and private charity (Health Care Financing Administration 1988, p. 19).

Ironically, although government policy has encouraged the use of nursing homes by tying government assistance for long-term care to this type of institution, it has simultaneously limited the supply of nursing home beds, thereby fostering queues and waiting lists. Many states have placed moratoria on new nursing home beds and have tightly regulated the total supply of such beds. Thus, Medicaid reimbursement policies, which foster nursing home living, and state regulation, which often discourages it, work at cross-purposes.

The result of this policy paradox can be seen not only in waiting lists but also in the development of "under the table" payments by families to nursing homes to gain entry for a family member. This means that access is provided to families with relatively more resources, which is hardly the intent of Medicaid, a program that supposedly predicates public assistance for long-term care on impoverishment.

Two other aspects of the current system should be noted. First, the system encourages asset transfers from the elderly to their children to feign family poverty. In effect, the nature of the system sends a signal to a middle-class family that if it can rearrange its assets so that instead of both parents and children being comfortable, but not wealthy, the parents appear broke and the children wealthy, then the parents receive public assistance (and the children receive a "windfall"). Of course, there are rules that limit this. The Medicare Catastrophic Act established a new national transfer of assets policy that puts minimum time requirements on the period between asset transfers and Medicaid eligibility. Resources disposed of for less than fair market value during the 30-month period prior to application for assistance are counted in one's stock of wealth (unless the transfer was to a spouse). Prior to the national rule, most states already had assets transfer rules. These types of rules have triggered all manner of creative "estate planning" that has the effect of circumventing the intent of the rules. Again, the reality of the situation is that the family that can afford the legal advice or is clever in devising "asset protection" plans is a "winner," relative to less sophisticated or less manipulative families. This does not appear to be a sound or a fair way to run a long-term care program. But in the absence of public or private social insurance mechanisms, and in a "spend your own money until you're broke" policy climate, it is reasonable to expect a lot of gaming.

The second feature of the system worth noting is the fact that many people who enter a nursing home are not on Medicaid when they enter, but "spend down" to Medicaid eligibility within a rather short time after entering. This occurs, of course, because nursing homes are expensive; it does not take too long at an annual cost that averages about $23,000 per year (and much higher in some urban areas) to deplete one's assets. A related problem is that Medicaid forces the income of the spouse of a nursing home patient down to a level that approximates the poverty level. Even with the new 1988 Medicare Catastrophic legislation, the spouse is only able to retain enough income to remain at 122 percent of the poverty line (starting in October 1989) and up to 150 percent of the poverty line by 1992.[2] Income above this level must be contributed by the spouse to the cost of the nursing home. Thus, not only does the household have to exhaust its assets to get the nursing home patient covered by Medicaid in the first place, but also the spouse, in effect, must agree to live on the borders of poverty on a continuous basis in order to receive assistance. Similarly, the personal needs allowance permitted the patient in a home is itself a paltry sum. Thus, it is important to understand that a problem with the current system is that there is no help to a family "on the way down" as it is exhausting its resources, and once the household is impoverished, it must stay that way to retain assistance.

Medicare's Share of the Financing

It was pointed out earlier that Medicare pays very little of the long-term care bill. The funding the program does make for this purpose consists basically of two parts. First, the program makes some "front end" nursing home payments for people entering what is termed a skilled nursing facility (SNF). This term is basically defined by the nature of the care and the qualifications of the personnel at the home (for example, does the home have registered nurses attending the patient on a regular basis, as opposed to aides and staff without nursing training?). Medicare covers up to 100 days of care in a skilled nursing facility (SNF), if it can be shown that the patient is on the road to recovery and is under a doctor's care. A coinsurance payment is required after the first 20 days of Medicare-covered SNF care. The deductible, currently set at $69 per day, often means that the elderly pay full cost of SNF care after the first 20 days.

Second, Medicare covers certain home care expenses. For example, it might cover the expenses associated with visiting nurses, physical therapy, or a wheelchair. Generally speaking, Medicare will not cover expenses at home that would be regarded as custodial. The Medicare home care benefit tends to be tied to skilled personnel under the direction of a physician or to equipment. The Medicare coverage for long-term care is another illustration of the linkage between insurance and the traditional medical model--insurance pays only if the condition is "curable."

Private Insurance's Role in Financing

Private insurance for long-term care has features similar to Medicare. It makes indemnity payments (*X* dollars per day) for nursing home care for a specified period (for example, two years), and either excludes home care or limits payments for it to skilled personnel who are part of a medical model of care. As noted below, private insurance has become more attractive to consumers recently, but there are still some services that are not well covered by either government or the private sector.

Increasingly, bills pile up for care that falls outside of the medical model. Many long-term care services are totally uninsured--adult day care, counseling for depression, companionship, transportation assistance, and home-delivered meals. As discussed in the following chapter, some of these needs are partially met through Title V government programs, but funding for such programs is limited and has been scaled back in recent years.

IS THIS SYSTEM APPROPRIATE FOR THE FUTURE ELDERLY?

The system is not appropriate for tomorrow's elderly population. There will be many more elderly persons requiring long-term care services in the future. Not only will the number of elderly persons increase dramatically but the number of elderly persons with limitations in activities of daily living and the number of elderly who will be living alone will likely increase disproportionately.

Figure 4.1 highlights some of the projections. In 1990 at least 6.5 million elderly persons probably will require some long-term care services. This represents about 20 percent of the total elderly population in the baseline projection. Assuming current rates of institutionalization, about 1.8 million will require nursing home care. Under the baseline projection assumptions, the number who will require some long-term care services rises to 9.2 million in 2010 and to 14.1 million in 2030. Thus, more than one in five elderly persons will require some services in 2010 and 2030 (the total number of elderly will be 41.2 million in 2010, and 64.4 in 2030, as shown in figure 2.1). Moreover, the number of elderly in institutions will rise to 3.0 million in 2010 and 4.3 million in 2030--an increase of 139 percent over the 1990 projection. As discussed earlier, the number of elderly persons doubles during the same period. Thus, the need for long-term care services will increase faster than the size of the elderly population between 1990 and 2030, if the baseline mortality and health assumptions are correct. If the optimistic mortality assumption is correct, and disability rates do not improve, the number of elderly requiring some long-term care services will be significantly greater. In this scenario, the bar labeled "optimistic mortality" in figure 4.1, 16.7 million elderly will need long-term care services in 2030.

This chart emphasizes the need for more focus on prevention of disability. If the health of the elderly improves at the same rate as mortality, the acceleration in the number of elderly requiring long-term care services because of increased longevity could be halted. (The number of elderly in need of long-term care services would increase by 112 percent, only slightly higher than the increase in the elderly population in this period.) This

Figure 4.1 **Potential Need For Long-Term Care Services**
For Persons Over Age 65, 1990-2030

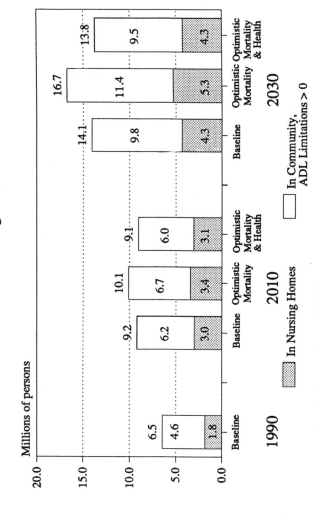

Source: Projections from The Urban Institute's DYNASIM model

scenario is depicted in the bars labeled "optimistic mortality and health" in figure 4.1.

Another factor likely to increase the proportion of elderly who will need formal care in the community is that many more elderly persons with need for services will be living alone in the future. Figure 4.2 highlights the change in living arrangements expected for the future elderly that was discussed in chapter 2. The number of elderly living alone under the baseline projection is expected to be 18.1 million in 2010 and 29.8 million in 2030, compared with 12.2 million in 1990. Thus, the proportion of elderly living alone in 2030 will increase to 46 percent, compared with 38 percent in 1990. As shown, the proportion of single elderly persons living with others in the 21st century is likely to decline significantly because of declines in marriage rates and birth rates, especially among the baby boom generation, and because of a strong preference of the elderly for living in their own homes.

Thus, maintenance of the current system of relying on family members for care at home is not likely to work for the future. There is likely to be an increased demand for formal in-home services. Moreover, maintenance of the current financing system would place an enormous burden on the Medicaid program, and it clearly would be inappropriate, given the portrait of the income position of the elderly presented earlier. There is likely to be tremendous diversity among the elderly with regard to resources. This means that there will be very substantial differences among the elderly in the ability to pay for long-term care themselves or to pay for the insurance that covers it.

The projections presented earlier indicate that the incomes of the elderly will continue to increase in real terms in the future, if not at the same rate as their predecessors. These projections also show that future income

Figure 4.2   Living Arrangements of the Elderly
Persons Over Age 65, 1990–2030

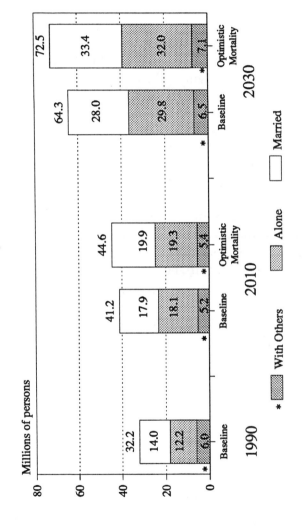

Source: Projections from The Urban
Institute's DYNASIM Model

growth will not eliminate the need for some type of gradu-
ated public assistance for lower-middle-income senior
citizens. Indeed, the projections show that many
unmarried elderly persons, particularly women, will be
especially vulnerable to the expenses of long-term care.
Figures 4.3 through 4.5 show the future distribution of
income among the elderly by marital status for 1990, 2010,
and 2030, respectively. These figures show that the vast
majority of single elderly persons will have incomes below
$10,000 in 1990 (in 1988 dollars), and very few will have
incomes that exceed $20,000. By 2030 (figure 4.5) about 80
percent of unmarried women and 60 percent of unmarried
men will have incomes below $20,000. Thus, if annual
income flow is used as a simple indicator of the ability to
afford nursing home care, the vast majority of single elderly persons still would not be able to afford the current
average annual cost of a nursing home (about $23,000).[3]
Moreover, because most of these persons are not expected
to have significant financial assets in the future, adding an
asset spend-down requirement would not change this
picture of affordability in any significant way.

The rising income of the elderly as a group, however,
does suggest that it would be unnecessary to subsidize all
senior citizens for long-term care. It indicates that many of
the elderly would be able to contribute to long-term care
costs, and many would be able to pay for less-expensive
in-home care services. Thus, the policy challenge is to find
ways to graduate public assistance for long-term care in a
way that relates it more clearly to need than the present
system without overcompensating the elderly as a group
in a way that discourages people from saving or insuring
themselves against the expenses of long-term care.

Figure 4.3 **Basic Income Distributions**
1990 Base case

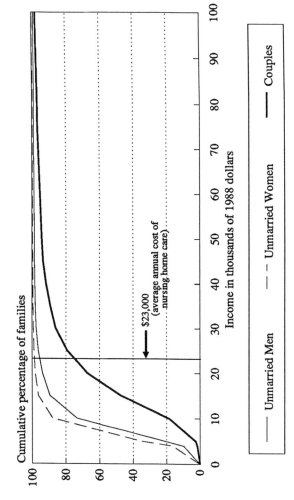

Source: DYNASIM projections
Note: Points on each line represent the cumulative percentage of families with income below that dollar amount.

Figure 4.4   **Basic Income Distributions**
2010 Base case

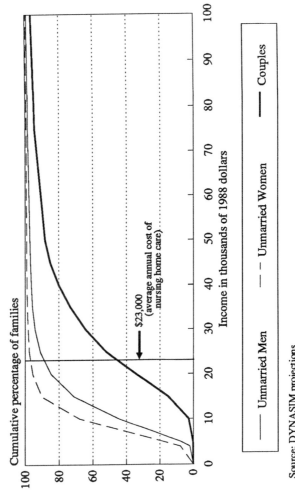

Source: DYNASIM projections
Note: Points on each line represent the cumulative percentage of families with income below that dollar amount.

Figure 4.5 **Basic Income Distributions**

2030 Base case

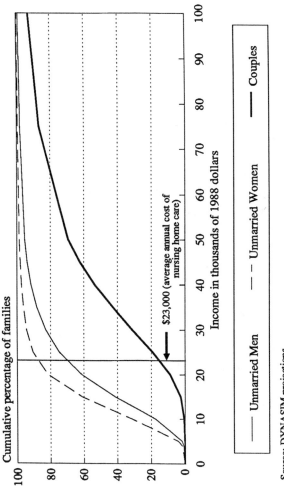

Source: DYNASIM projections

Note: Points on each line represent the cumulative percentage of families with income below that dollar amount.

GOALS FOR ADJUSTING THE SYSTEM
TO MEET THE CHANGING NEEDS
OF THE ELDERLY

There are several avenues that must be pursued to adjust to the changing long-term care needs of the elderly. The place to begin is with efforts to prevent disability in the first place. As emphasized earlier, even a modest decrease in disability rates will significantly dampen the need for institutionalized long-term care services. Very few health care dollars are devoted to research that could prevent, or at least postpone the diseases of aging. Of the $145 billion spent on health care for the elderly in the United States, less than 0.5 percent was invested in research (Carpenter 1989, p. 86). Second, alternative approaches to care delivery must be considered. The focus here should be care in the least restrictive (and least costly) environment possible. Third, alternative approaches to financing long-term care services must be offered. As the population becomes aware that the risk for long-term care services faces all elderly people and that current insurance mechanisms do not cover this type of health care very well, more should be willing to pay for long-term care insurance. Moreover, these financing strategies should allow the elderly to plan far in advance for long-term care services. Their incomes tend to be highest just after retirement and lowest when long-term care services are needed. Thus, the financing plan should provide a mechanism that allows the elderly to spread their share of the cost of long-term care over the retirement period.

Preventing Disability

There is a role for the concept of prevention in strategic planning for long-term care. The impact of prevention can be realized at multiple levels: through a reduction in the incidence of chronic and disabling conditions, reduction in the severity of their debilitating effects, and reduction in the magnitude of dependence on long-term care services. Given projected service demands of the growing elderly population, the high cost of institutional care, and finite resources available to meet the demand, every incentive is present to explore this avenue. Past experience demonstrates, however, that preventive efforts can only be as effective as the extent to which they are appropriately targeted and efficiently administered. Particular attention therefore must be directed at identifying groups for whom the greatest benefit can be expected and at approaches that have the greatest potential for producing measurable impact.

The overall approach toward prevention, within the context of long-term care, also must reflect a cognizance of attitudes toward aging and chronic illness and of the extent to which a preventive mindset is, or can be made, compatible with these attitudes and with other priorities of the health care system. Prevention, as a mainline health care approach, has not traditionally achieved the prominence, recognition, or infusion of resources that curative intervention has achieved. Nor is the manner in which the health care delivery system is structured and financed particularly conducive to the practice of preventive health care.

Most commonly, the point of entry into the health care system occurs when an individual is already experiencing signs of illness. This is in part attitudinal, a function of health-care-seeking behavior. But even those who might be inclined to seek preventive services are sometimes dissuaded by financial considerations, because these services often are not covered under health insurance policies. The underinsured and the uninsured delay seeking medical attention even longer.

When contact with a health provider does occur, there is a financial disincentive on the part of the provider toward devoting time to "preventive functions" (for example, health teaching) for which he or she will not be reimbursed. Moreover, the curative focus of the medical model, under which the health care system operates, "rewards" in direct relation to the process of *diagnosis* of a disease, *treatment* of the involved organ system, and *cure* of the patient.

How does this mesh with the long-term-care patient whose problems are chronic and multisystemic? Clearly not very well. The curative mindset is even less responsive to the host of nonmedical variables that contribute to the chronicity and severity of illness in the elderly, such as safety hazards in the environment, poor nutritional intake, and mobility problems. Most importantly, these factors are overlooked when they are still "risk factors" and have not yet been expressed as part of an illness state.

Also, despite the promotion of community-based care delivery and the popularity of terms such as "case management" and "comprehensive services," reimbursement continues to heavily favor institutional care and care for discrete medical conditions. Even for elderly people known to have some degree of illness or disability, the services that could keep them from needing to enter institutional settings, or that could keep them out once discharged (that is, services that are "preventive" with respect to need for institutional care) are subject to exceedingly stringent criteria of "medical necessity" and often are met with denial by third-party payers.

An intrinsic paradox becomes evident here, given concern over rising long-term care expenditures: The high costs associated with long-term care are explained primarily by the utilization patterns of a very small segment of the elderly population--those who require institutional placement and/or frequent hospital admissions. *It follows, then, that even a modest redistribution of the resources available to the elderly, directed at those who are currently healthy but who are at significant risk for becoming "high cost cases," has the potential to be more cost-effective than ultimately treating them in institutions.*

In a later section of this chapter on alternative approaches to care delivery, considerable attention is given to care settings that have the potential to compensate for many of the risk factors cited above, and that may prevent a degree of dependence on institutional settings. It will be argued that when care is managed with proficiency through all stages of illness, without interruption or fragmentation, and when it is delivered in an appropriate setting, the incidence of complications and exacerbations and the extent of disability can be controlled, or its progression can be slowed. In summary, prevention efforts are highly compatible with the objectives of long-term care strategy: maintaining health status, independence, and quality of life for the elderly. If prevention is to be an effective component of long-term care, more needs to be understood about where the efforts should be most intensively targeted, and then effort should focus on ensuring that the services are accessible and affordable to those identified in need.

Improving the Delivery of Care

As policies are being shaped in response to projected long-term care needs, it is vital to critically examine prevailing service delivery approaches. Out of this process, creative strategies can be developed to achieve greater congruence between anticipated health care needs and the range of service options made available. In fact, there is a growing body of experience with a number of alternative delivery approaches that suggests that this "fit" can be improved. From a policy perspective, the challenge is to develop a rational approach to integrating these services into the mainstream of health care delivery, and into regulatory and financing systems, in a manner that will produce optimal health outcomes without producing runaway spending.

In developing policies aimed at ensuring access to appropriate long-term care, it is necessary therefore (1) to define operationally "appropriate" long-term care services, so that the specific nature and scope of care requirements of this population are considered; (2) to view long-term care within the context of the overall patterns of health care resource use of the chronically ill; and (3) to identify opportunities to tailor the intensity and scope of services to match the intensity and scope of needs more precisely. The outcomes of this process can be to minimize inefficient utilization patterns, to minimize the degree of dependency on long-term care, and to maintain the health and independence of these individuals at the highest possible level.

Defining Appropriate Care

The notion of "appropriate" care has become increasingly complex and difficult to specify: Who should render the care, in what setting should it be delivered, how much and what kinds of care are to be considered "medically necessary?" Several trends contribute to this uncertainty. They include the promotion of community versus institutional care; the reduction in hospital admissions and length of stay under prospective payment; the proliferation of ambulatory care centers for all levels of treatment; the expansion of the scope of nurse practitioners and physician's assistants, as well as the increased delegation of skilled duties to technical personnel (for example, licensed practical nurses); and the emphasis on greater assumption of responsibility for performance of health-related tasks by informal care givers and patients themselves. Generally speaking, the least intensive medical setting or delivery approach that can avert a catastrophic health event has been adopted as the minimal standard to determine that care has been appropriate.

A factor that limits the precision of determinations about the appropriateness of long-term care is the persistent adherence to a medical orientation in determining what care is "necessary." The inherent paradox in this mindset is that many if not most needs of long-term care recipients are not strictly medical in nature. Yet nonmedical intervention and support (to individuals and their primary care givers) are rarely acknowledged as legitimate, mainline, long-term care services.

Unlike the sophisticated protocols that have been established to monitor diagnostic and therapeutic regimens in acute hospital care, uniformly accepted criteria have not been promulgated in the long-term care arena. Such standards would need to incorporate not only medical criteria but also measures of improvement or deterioration in functional, mental, and emotional status, as well as the extent to which care givers are able to sustain their own capacities to meet the individual's needs. Lacking such inclusive and sensitive measures of appropriateness, segments of the long-term care population can be overlooked, in effect, insofar as they experience less visible negative effects and more insidious deterioration or debilitation as the result of a poor match between needs and services.

Considering Total Health Care Needs

Chronically ill people are highly prevalent consumers of acute hospital resources and often enter into a "revolving door" pattern of hospital use. Each admission places the individual at risk for iatrogenic complications and deterioration of physical, mental, and emotional status. This, in turn, leaves the individual more susceptible to subsequent illness or injury and to intensified dependence on long-term care. Care-giver burdens also increase with each episode, rendering these family members or friends more vulnerable to "burnout," a proximate cause of many rehospitalizations, and even institutionalization, of the chronically ill.

The potential for resumption and continuation of independent living in the community diminishes precipitously following serial hospitalizations or an institutional placement. Finally, it should be emphasized that even in persons who are free of a chronic condition, it is most often the occurrence of an acute event that does not resolve satisfactorily in the subacute phase that precipitates the onset of chronicity and long-term care dependence.

For a variety of reasons the current health care system fosters a revolving door between acute and long-term care services. Chronically ill patients are frequently hospitalized during acute health need episodes. Often their conditions do not warrant the full array of high-tech, labor-intensive services found in an acute care hospital, but inpatient admission is the only widely available option that offers a controlled setting for sustained periods of medical monitoring. Hospitalization is also frequently the only route to reimbursement under either public or private payment systems.

Some chronically ill patients do become gravely ill, and ultimately require the full intensity of hospital services. But not infrequently this scenario follows a lengthy, frustrating, and unsuccessful attempt to orchestrate and gain access to necessary services in the community. Virtually all hospitals have backlogs of patients who can and should be discharged, but cannot be released because the necessary community services or skilled nursing facility beds cannot be secured.

Still other patients are discharged from hospital care with arrangements for home health care, only to find that they and their care givers are ill-prepared to manage often highly complex care requirements. Assistance and instruction by a visiting nurse may be available only one or two hours per week, and often only after a delay of several days following discharge because of coordination and/or staffing problems. Physicians are similarly frustrated in their efforts to manage patient care through slow and inefficient mail correspondence with home health providers. Nurses are faced with managing high-tech procedures in patients' homes, with little backup and with major concerns for patient safety.

Given this inextricable link between acute and long-term care, preventive opportunities become evident. Through reduction of the need to hospitalize and through highly skillful management of acute and subacute care requirements, the risk of long-term debilitation could be reduced.

Adjusting Services to Need--Innovative Methods

The set of innovations in the delivery system analyzed in this section offers degrees of alternatives to 24-hour institutional care on the one hand, and to limited one- to two-hour in-home nursing visits on the other. These options furnish various packages of medical services and social supports that are tailored more precisely to the reality of needs of long-term-care patients and their care givers. They can be viewed as potential substitutes for the less efficient, less appropriate care delivery that would result from use of only traditional service settings to attempt to deliver a comparable range of services.

Several of the following approaches possess analogous features, but each maintains a slightly different focus in terms of philosophy, target population, or service approach: cooperative care, day hospital, adult day health care (ADHC), subacute care alternatives (SCA), comprehensive outpatient rehabilitation facilities (CORFs), transitional care units, hospital-hotels, and community care organizations. Many of these options are being tested and are proving to be not only more responsive to needs but also more cost-effective.

COOPERATIVE CARE

A cooperative care unit is an inpatient unit that is used in lieu of traditional hospitalization or as a substitute for a portion of an acute care stay. "Co-op care" patients meet all the same criteria used in admission to an acute care hospital with the following contingencies: (1) the patient must have a "care partner" who can stay with him/her throughout the admission for as many hours per day as the patient's condition necessitates; (2) the patient must be able to ambulate or be mobile by wheelchair; and (3) patients with highly unstable conditions or "intensive care" requirements are excluded.

The distinguishing feature of cooperative care is that patients and their care partners are educated, from the very minute they walk in, and are made responsible for sharing in the care requirements, as opposed to relinquishing of virtually all responsibility to staff members, as in a traditional hospital. Instead of breeding dependency, co-op care fosters self-reliance and focuses on preparedness for managing care at home, by way of a very sophisticated educational program. Patients "room in" with their care partners. Electric beds are not used, nor are rooms equipped with wall oxygen and suction, as would be found in every hospital room (portable equipment is brought to the rooms only as needed). The objective is to simulate the home environment and to find out while the patient is still in cooperative care what needs for medical devices and ancillary equipment should be planned for at home. There are no staff persons stationed on patient floors. All nursing care, assessment, and treatment is provided in a centralized therapeutic center. Telephones and emergency bells connect each room to the staffed area.

Average length of stay in cooperative care is four days. Seventy-five percent of patients take their own medications. Virtually all patients and their care partners eat their meals in the cafeteria. Costs are said to be one-third lower than for traditional hospitalization. Staffing levels are markedly lower than those found on a typical hospital unit. Patient and family satisfaction is generally higher and anxiety lower than in traditional inpatient settings, and health outcomes experienced in co-op care appear favorable.

At least 19 cooperative care units are in operation nationwide, the largest of which is at New York University Medical Center in New York City. The approach has been implemented with particular success for medical patients with complex conditions that will likely require a high degree of patient involvement in a long-term management process. The key to its effectiveness appears to be in the manner in which it prepares patients and care givers to manage care requirements effectively, safely, and confidently once the patients leave the cooperative care setting.

THE DAY HOSPITAL

The day hospital approach has been operationalized for primarily three types of patients: psychiatric, rehabilitation, and oncology. For certain patients within these groups, the availability of a day hospital means averting the need to be hospitalized or substantially reducing the inpatient length of stay that would be required otherwise. Patients become eligible for day hospital treatment when the stability of their condition permits, if adequate supports and a care giver are present in the home, and transportation can be arranged.

Instead of 24-hour staffing coverage required for an inpatient unit, the day hospital is staffed for 8 hours per day (often for five rather than seven days per week). During this time patients receive services of fully comparable intensity and scope to those they would receive as inpatients. Patients are monitored and assessed daily and their treatments adjusted accordingly.

Good Samaritan Medical Center in Phoenix and Moss Rehabilitation Hospital in Philadelphia operate two of the well-established day hospital programs. The distribution of such programs nationwide, however, has remained highly scattered. Blue Cross and some HMOs are the only insurers, to date, who have fully recognized the day hospital approach for rehabilitation patients, thus seriously limiting the number of hospitals willing to initiate such programs.

Evaluations of day hospital programs have been able to document improved patient and family satisfaction, markedly lower costs, and comparable levels of patient compliance and clinical outcomes to those of their inpatient counterparts.

ADULT DAY HEALTH CARE

The adult day health care model (ADHC) is distinguished from the social day care model by the addition of a health care component. The service is generally directed at the elderly population and particularly at individuals considered at highest risk for institutionalization.

ADHC is intended to maintain or improve the functional status of frail persons to enable them to remain in their homes and communities, in as independent and healthy condition as possible. It uses the dual approach of seeking to preserve the strength of the family unit (the primary care givers of the elderly) and to prevent physical and mental deterioration in elderly persons through therapeutic activity, socialization, and health education, monitoring, and maintenance intervention by nursing and support personnel. A typical staff/registrant ratio is 1:4, with one-half of those staff members being trained professionals.

Referrals are generated from hospital discharge planners, private physicians, social service agencies, and self-referrals. The ADHC population is quite heterogeneous. A given facility may care for persons with chronic cardiovascular disease, others with Alzheimer's disease, and still others with neuromuscular disorders. Registrants range from having almost no impairment to severe disability, from acute convalescence to prolonged chronicity. The duration of attendance varies from less than one month to more than one year.

A study in California compared costs between skilled nursing facility/intensive care facility (SNF/ICF) certifiable enrollees who participated in ADHC and regular

SNF/ICF residents. It found that ADHC institutional-level clients average $456 less per month in MediCal costs, for an annual saving of $5,472 per person (Capitman 1984). On a national scale, the Veterans Administration is presently engaged in a major prospective study of the cost-effectiveness of ADHC as a substitute for institutional care and its efficacy in improving health outcomes.

Adult day care is available in every state, and it is estimated that between 1,500 and 1,700 such programs operate nationwide. State-to-state variations in availability and use of ADHCs are quite pronounced, relating to rates of Medicaid reimbursement and regulations that determine the sites at which they are allowed to operate. Some states permit ADHCs to be free-standing, hospital-based, or based out of skilled nursing facilities. Other states limit their operation to skilled nursing facility sites only. Another factor expected to affect use of ADHCs is the federal legislation that has been introduced, which would make Medicare a source of reimbursement for this service.

THE SUBACUTE CARE ALTERNATIVE

The subacute care alternative (SCA) represents a new service approach for patients who continue to have complex and intensive care requirements in the period immediately following hospital discharge. This model was developed by the Economic and Social Research Institute in Reston, Virginia, under a grant from The Robert Wood Johnson Foundation. Beginning in 1990, it will be demonstrated in two sites, in Washington, D.C., and New York State.

Development of this approach was undertaken in response to concerns that the transition toward community-based care has left certain "gaps" in access to needed aftercare, most often and most adversely affecting the elderly. The opportunity to prevent repeat hospitalizations (for example, resulting from postdischarge complications) and premature long-term care dependence by optimizing recovery potential during the subacute phase constitutes the primary focus of this approach.

Physicians also have expressed the view that this setting could serve as a highly suitable alternative to hospital admission for selected medical patients who require periods of close professional supervision to adjust treatment and monitor response, but who do not require 24-hour services in an acute care hospital. Also, certain hospitalized patients, who might otherwise experience protracted inpatient stays, potentially could be released from the hospital sooner, given the availability of intensive SCA follow-up.

The SCA is believed to hold the potential to deliver this level of care with more efficacy and efficiency than can be attained through existing ambulatory approaches, for those patients with particularly complex cases. Two features of the model are seen as essential to realizing this potential: (1) offering a full day program of care, of an intensity and scope expressly tailored to the needs of the subacute patient, on a strictly time-limited basis, and (2) targeting patient groups that possess the highest intensity or complexity of care requirements, who are at risk of receiving inadequate community-based aftercare and to experience adverse outcomes with subsequent repeat use of costly, high-tech services or even premature, avoidable dependence on long-term care.

The full range of services and complement of professionals is to be made available on-site, to allow for sustained patient monitoring and administration of multiple treatments such as intravenous therapies, physical therapy, frequent wound care, and complex dressing changes. An interdisciplinary team is responsible for carrying out the posthospital plan of care in accordance with the attending physician's treatment goals for each patient. Opportunities for the proficient practice of case management and patient/family education are maximized by this central, consistent setting for the delivery of subacute care. Care givers are supported by being able to maintain employment outside the home during this intensive recovery period of their family member.

For postacute patients who otherwise might be referred to a home health agency following hospitalization, the SCA may be an alternative to home health care when (1) home health care cannot provide the frequency and/or intensity of care required, or cannot deliver the therapies in such a manner as to provide safe and optimal benefits of the prescribed treatment; and (2) the therapeutic needs of the patient are such that use of home care becomes excessively inefficient in terms of cost and use of already scarce personnel.

COMPREHENSIVE OUTPATIENT REHABILITATION FACILITIES

Comprehensive outpatient rehabilitation facilities (CORFs) were established under a federal initiative to provide restorative rehabilitation services to chronically debilitated adults over the age of 65. CORFs were established under Section 933 of the Omnibus Reconciliation Act of 1980, which amended several sections of the Social Security Act. They are reimbursed under Part B of Medicare. CORF programs seek to extend rehabilitation services to those who are being served in an excessively fragmented or incomplete manner through other settings, such as hospital-based outpatient physical therapy departments. The objective is one of preventing or delaying the need for institutional care.

Programs may be sponsored by residential health facilities, hospitals, certified home health agencies, or office-based practitioners. Their distribution nationwide is not uniform; they are highly concentrated on the East Coast, particularly in Florida.

CORFs treat patients with moderate to severe impairments, often those who are suffering from neurological injuries with long-term impairments. Examples of the conditions treated include traumatic brain injury, post-cerebrovascular-accident (stroke) conditions, postsurgical aneurysm, anoxia secondary to trauma or cardiopulmonary arrest, and postsurgical hemorrhage. Therapy must be provided to each patient at least three times weekly and must include, at a minimum, physician services, physical therapy, and social and psychological services.

TRANSITIONAL CARE

This is care provided on an inpatient basis in a limited number of facilities. Such units are created when particular hospital beds, or hospital-based skilled nursing beds, are designated by the provider institution to provide this "step down" level of care following the strictly defined "medically acute" phase of an illness. Staffing requirements are lowered, but the benefits of 24-hour monitoring and availability of ancillary and emergency services make this an attractive service alternative for individuals whose conditions are no longer acute but who are not yet stable enough to safely leave an inpatient setting.

The extent of formally designated transitional care across the nation is not well known, largely because of extreme variations in the terminology used to identify such services and because of regional variations in the manner in which "medically necessary acute care" and, in turn, "postacute care," are defined. The Prospective Payment Assessment Commission has been the sponsor of a national study to determine more precisely the nature and extent of the development of transitional care beds. The preliminary finding is that the amount of subacute care in hospitals is small and varies little across the nation. Only 5.2 percent of hospitals that are not designated as "swing bed" hospitals (those that have beds formally designated for use as *either* hospital or skilled nursing beds) provided any care identified as subacute care (Rivlin and Wiener 1988).

HOSPITAL-HOTEL

The hospital-hotel is a further step down from transitional care. In this model, a hotel is structurally attached to a hospital facility, where ambulatory postsurgical and subacute medical patients can convalesce at a fraction of the cost of continued hospitalization. The iatrogenic hazards associated with a hospital stay are thereby reduced. Yet given the proximity to the hospital, physicians can continue to closely monitor the postacute courses of their patients and to prescribe treatments accordingly. This may be particularly beneficial for older individuals who reside a great distance from the hospital where they received acute care and who would be at substantial risk if their condition suddenly worsened at home.

Only paramedics are stationed in the hotel building to facilitate expeditious care and contact with hospital personnel if an emergency arises. While housed in the hotel, individuals have a daily routine of getting dressed, having meals in the restaurant, and attending educational programs or therapy.

The hospital-hotel concept has been operationalized in a limited number of sites across the country. Interest in this approach has been growing recently, in recognition of its potential for achieving cost reduction and improved health benefits. Plans to build a 100-bed facility in New Haven, Connecticut are nearing completion, and a number of other sites are demonstrating interest in conducting institution-specific feasibility planning.

COMMUNITY CARE ORGANIZATIONS

Perhaps the most inclusive approach to long-term care management that has been developed to date is On-Lok's Community Care Organization for Dependent Adults (CCODA). Originated in San Francisco, the model is now being replicated at selected sites across the nation. The CCODA represents a risk-based, consolidated model of coordinated long-term care. It delivers all services directly, as opposed to a brokerage model in which a case manager coordinates existing community services on behalf of the frail elderly person. It is also distinguished from health maintenance organizations, primarily because only frail elderly persons who are chronically ill and state-certified as needing full-time nursing home care can be enrolled.

The On-Lok staff directly provides primary medical care, skilled nursing care, physical therapy, occupational therapy, recreational therapy, social services, nutritional counseling, adult day health care, social day care, post-discharge planning, transportation, meals, personal care, and in-home care. Professionals under contract provide specialized medical services, and facilities under contract provide acute hospital and skilled nursing facility care, diagnostic testing, and medication. The program also coordinates and operates various housing options, including respite care.

The goal of the On-Lok program has been to bridge inappropriate separations of medical, social, and support services and to create a single entity for the management and delivery of all health and health-related long-term services for this frail elderly population. From its inception, the program has been conducted with highly systematic attention to research. Among their many findings, evaluators have been able to document significant reductions in both acute hospital days and in skilled nursing facility days for their enrollees, compared with control groups.

REQUIREMENTS FOR SUCCESSFUL ADJUSTMENTS AND INNOVATIONS

The attention to research and systematic planning for replication evident in the On-Lok experience may serve as a model for other innovative models of care delivery. Other models have experienced some degree of constraint in their growth and level of acceptance, because of the following factors: (1) The most salient problem is inadequate, poorly structured, or even absent reimbursement mechanisms for alternative care models. The cause here is that third-party payers resist waiving restrictions to include new services and balk at establishing discrete rates commensurate with service intensity without a priori evidence of their cost-effectiveness and savings. (2) Another set of problems involves regulatory constraints, lack of "enabling" categories of licensure, and discontinuities in the interpretation of regulations. These impediments are attributable largely to reluctance on the part of regulators to develop, promote, and devote resources to new alternatives without a firm basis for establishing need and without methodologies for projecting fiscal impacts. (3) Compounding the constraints on planning is the very limited base of scientifically sound data and information that documents, in quantitative terms, the efficacy and efficiency of these approaches and the extent of unmet, or inefficiently met, health care needs under traditional approaches (this lack of data is largely responsible for points 1 and 2 above). Without highly unified, systematic efforts to demonstrate and study alternative care approaches, a lack of generalizable, valid, and reliable results will continue to impede progress. (4) Lack of uniform availability of alternative service approaches, coupled with a lack of physician and patient knowledge about them and deeply ingrained societal and personal beliefs and attitudes about how, where, and by whom health care services should be rendered, has resulted in the persistent tendency of clients to refer to and use established, known entities. (5) Finally, the system is hobbled by the reluctance of providers to establish these alternative service approaches--a result of all of the above factors. Thus, the circle is closed, and the constraints are perpetuated.

Breaking the cycle of constraints that have impeded the development and growth of potentially more appropriate approaches to long-term care must begin with the development of a rational basis for policymaking. This, in turn, can be established only through research and demonstration/replication initiatives that generate data and document the degree of efficacy and efficiency attainable under each approach. Given finite resources for such initiatives, it may be necessary first to focus on the more precise identification of factors that place individuals at highest risk of long-term care dependency, not only for institutionalization but also for serial hospitalizations, as discussed previously. Once those factors are better understood, it follows that approaches with the potential to reduce, eliminate, or compensate for these factors should receive priority attention.

The integration of new service alternatives into the health care delivery system requires establishing appropriate linkages among them, as well as between them and existing sources of care delivery. All affected parties need to be educated about their appropriate use.

The solution to long-term care problems clearly does not lie in the simple addition of skilled nursing beds, expansion of home health capabilities, or tolerance of long-term care needs being managed in acute care hospitals. Yet even the alternatives described in this chapter as having the potential to serve long-term care patients more appropriately can be effective only to the extent to which they are properly targeted at those patients who will derive measurable benefit and who would be at risk otherwise for missing essential services.

An effective solution requires standards against which "measurable benefits" can be measured with more precision than the "absence of a serious negative health event." Only when a strictly "medical mindset" can be expanded to include nonmedical considerations in decision-making about standards for "essential" services will it be possible to proactively steer the course of long-term clients away from dependency.

As discussed in the following chapters, there are also several new approaches to reorganize long-term care and to integrate it with other health, housing, and social services. These models are designed to redress the fragmentation in our health care system--between acute and long-term care and between the delivery system as a whole and the financing of services. Innovative systems include the social health maintenance organization (SHMO), in which a single provider organization assumes responsibility for ambulatory, acute inpatient, rehabilitation, nursing home, home health, and personal care services under a prospectively determined budget, and continuing care retirement communities, which provide housing, health care, and social services to senior citizens.

New Sources of Financing for Long-Term Care

To a large extent, innovations in care delivery will not occur without innovations in financing mechanisms. The private sector is not likely to respond to demands for alternative care arrangements unless these services are affordable for a large segment of the elderly population. This section examines new ways of generating financing for long-term care. It addresses the challenges, noted earlier, in finding ways to generalize risk and in breaking the linkage between long-term care and poverty. Various insurance mechanisms are addressed. This section also reviews possibilities for allowing the elderly to tap their illiquid housing assets to help defray the cost of long-term care, but in a way that protects this asset throughout their lifetime.

PRIVATE LONG-TERM CARE INSURANCE

One of the most promising areas of reform in the financing of long-term care is the development of a more mature market for long-term care insurance. As noted earlier, private insurance for long-term care covers only about 1 percent of the total nursing home bill, and it provides little in the way of home care coverage. The market for long-term care insurance is changing rapidly, however, and it would be a mistake to judge the long-range potential of such insurance from the embryonic stage of development of the market in the mid-1980s.

Today's elderly are a risk-averse group, judging by the number who purchase health insurance policies to cover acute care expenditures that are not covered through Medicare. In 1988, for example, 70 percent of the elderly had private insurance in addition to Medicare coverage.[4] Whereas about a third of the elderly had this insurance through their current or previous employers, 37 percent were purchasing health insurance privately. Moreover, the majority of the elderly with employer-provided plans were contributing to premiums.

There is every indication that the elderly have not purchased insurance for long-term care because they believe that these needs are covered through current insurance and because the "first generation" long-term care insurance policies were inadequate. But there is also every indication that this situation is changing quickly. More and more of the elderly realize that long-term care services are not covered through their health insurance policies or Medicare and that long-term care insurance policies are rapidly improving.

The early versions of private long-term care insurance have had a number of flaws that limited their attractiveness to consumers. Restrictions included prior hospitalization requirements and limited benefits for custodial care (help with cooking, bathing, and dressing), and no inflation adjustments for the daily cost of care. Many newer policies, however, have lifted many of these restrictions in exchange for a higher price tag. Real protection is expensive. Based on policies available in 1989, moderate protection requires about $733 per year if purchased at age 65, $1,350 if purchased at age 70, and $2,500 if purchased at age 75 (Findlay 1989, p. 65).[5] This policy would include a $50-a-day benefit, a 20-day deductible, inflation adjustments, and no requirement of prior hospitalization. Moreover, industry analysts maintain that premiums will come down if more employers offered LTC coverage as part of group health plans.

Although the product is improving, there are still some concerns about the extent to which consumers will purchase the offerings of insurance companies. These concerns include the issue of affordability, the lack of understanding about the need for this coverage, and the issue of adverse risk selection and moral hazard (the coverage may be appealing only to those who deem themselves likely to use it in the foreseeable future, thereby loading the plans with "bad risks").

Consistent with the theme of this chapter--the development of policy steps that can overcome barriers, lower costs, and improve services--are a variety of issues and options that affect attempts to increase the appeal and use of long-term care insurance.

The issue of affordability of long-term care insurance has been the focus of much debate. A recent study by the Brookings Institution indicated that by the period 2016 to 2020, 26 to 45 percent of the elderly would be able to afford long-term care insurance but that this insurance would finance only 7 to 12 percent of nursing home expenditures and would have only a modest downward impact on Medicaid outlays (Rivlin and Wiener 1988).

A close examination of the assumptions underlying these projections indicates that they are very restrictive. Indeed, the findings can be read in an encouraging light if one concludes that at least a fourth--and possibly half--of the elderly would purchase such insurance under these highly restrictive assumptions. The Brookings study assumes that people may buy an individual indemnity policy at the age of 67, including up to six years of nursing home coverage for those meeting a 3-day prior hospitalization requirement, after a 100-day deductible. Individuals are assumed to buy the insurance only if it can be purchased with 5 percent or less of their income and if they have at least $10,000 in nonhousing assets (no spend-down of assets is required).

The critical assumptions are that people who would have to spend more than 5 percent of their incomes on long-term care insurance or have less than $10,000 in financial assets cannot afford it (or would not purchase it).[6] These are fairly rigid (and relatively low) thresholds. For example, it was shown earlier that many of the elderly are not likely to have significant financial assets, but many will enjoy significant growth in real income from pensions and Social Security. Moreover, some of today's most vulnerable groups are likely to have higher rates of growth in income than others, a factor that will reduce the disparities in ability to pay. For example, the frail elderly are expected to be much better off than their predecessors starting in 2010 (see chapter 3, figure 3.1). This group comprises those who benefited from the strong economy of the 1960s and 1970s. Their Social Security and pension benefits will reflect strong growth in real earnings during their working years. Beginning in 2030, these projections also show significant strides in the income position of elderly single women. At this time many more unmarried women (single, divorced, and widowed) will have pensions, and they will have earned significant Social Security benefits (even with reductions enacted in the recent amendments in Social Security) because of stronger attachments to the labor force. The projections also showed a strong income position for married couples.

Thus, a broad group of elderly persons might be able to afford long-term care policies in the future. If some concept of discretionary income after the basic necessities such as food, clothing, and out-of-pocket outlays for acute medical care, along with taxes, were subtracted from gross income, the affordability threshold would be substantially higher than 5 percent for many elderly families.

Tables 4.1 and 4.2 illustrate the effect of purchasing the type of insurance described above on the incomes of elderly persons in 2030. Each table shows the effects of a different level of premium--$720 per year and $2,400 per year (in 1988 dollars)--to show a range of possibilities. At the lower premium rate--the approximate cost of a moderate level of insurance purchased at age 65--about 48 percent of all older persons could afford this premium for less than 5 percent of their gross annual income, and another 23 percent could afford it for less than 10 percent of their income. But at the higher premium rate--the approximate cost of purchasing the same coverage at age 75--only 13 percent of the elderly could afford it with less than 5 percent of their income, and another 15 percent could afford it with less than 10 percent of their income.

Affordability declines with age. Only 2 percent of persons 85 and older could finance insurance premiums of $2,400 per year with less than 5 percent of their incomes. In fact, this premium would represent 20 percent or more of the incomes of the vast majority of persons in this age group. This table dramatically illustrates the importance of planning for this potential expense. The earlier the insurance is purchased, the less expensive the annual premium. Older persons who can afford these payments in the early part of their retirement should be encouraged to do so.

These projections also illustrate that insurance is not the only answer to the long-term care financing problem. Insurance premiums no doubt will increase in real terms. Thus, the $720 premium shown would be lower than the real cost of insurance in 2030. Although many argue that increased participation in this market will decrease premiums, is is not likely to completely offset real increases in the cost of trained personnel, facilities, and so on over the next 40 years. Thus, real insurance costs, even when purchased at age 65 or earlier, probably will fall between the two levels illustrated. And, for many older people these costs would be prohibitive. Encouragement of the private insurance market thus should be coupled with policies

Table 4.1   LONG-TERM CARE INSURANCE FOR THE ELDERLY AS
A PERCENTAGE OF PERSONAL INCOME IN 2030
(BASE-CASE SCENARIO) WITH PREMIUMS SET AT $720
ANNUALLY (in 1988 dollars)

Percentage of Income	Age					Total
	65-69	70-74	75-79	80-84	85+	
	Thousands of Persons					
0-5%	11,437	9,295	5,395	2,991	1,504	30,623
0-2.5%	8,285	6,312	3,114	1,652	651	20,014
2.5-5%	3,152	2,983	2,282	1,339	854	10,609
5-10%	3,486	3,617	3,021	2,396	1,952	14,471
5-7.5%	1,791	1,783	1,225	972	849	6,621
7.5-10%	1,694	1,834	1,796	1,424	1,103	7,850
10-20%	2,375	2,751	2,890	2,670	3,756	14,441
10-15%	1,618	1,872	1,935	1,935	2,607	9,967
15-20%	756	879	955	735	1,149	4,474
20%-up	642	828	925	908	1,530	4,833
Total	17,939	16,490	12,231	8,966	8,742	64,368

that allow the elderly to increase their incomes and supportive government policies that work in tandem with
private long-term care insurance.

HOME EQUITY CONVERSION

There is increasing interest in making it possible for the
elderly to easily tap accrued personal assets to contribute
to their medical expenses. Home equity conversion is one

Table 4.1 *continued*

Percentage of Income	Age					Total
	65-69	70-74	75-79	80-84	85+	
Percentage Distribution						
0-5%	64	56	44	33	17	48
0-2.5%	46	38	26	18	7	31
2.5-5%	18	18	19	15	10	17
5-10%	19	22	25	27	22	23
5-7.5%	10	11	10	11	10	10
7.5-10%	9	11	15	16	13	12
10-20%	13	17	24	30	43	22
10-15%	9	11	16	22	30	16
15-20%	4	5	8	8	13	7
20%-up	4	5	8	10	18	8
Total	100	100	100	100	100	100

Note: Calculations show the cost of the long-term care insurance (set at $720 annually) as a percentage of *person-level* income. In other words, insurance is calculated as a percentage of family income for unmarried persons but as a percentage of only one-half of family income for married couples.

way to create additional private cash flow that can be channeled to health and long-term care, or to facilitate the delivery of care in less expensive settings. As discussed in chapter 6, it can provide the potential for some elderly to modify their current dwellings so that they can stay in their communities and avoid the cost of long-term care

Table 4.2   LONG-TERM CARE INSURANCE FOR THE ELDERLY
AS A PERCENTAGE OF PERSONAL INCOME IN 2030
(BASE-CASE SCENARIO) WITH PREMIUMS SET AT
$2,400 ANNUALLY (in 1988 dollars)

Percentage of Income	Age					Total
	65-69	70-74	75-79	80-84	85+	
	Thousands of Persons					
0-5%	3,680	2,674	1,234	469	207	8,264
5-10%	5,869	4,673	2,658	1,589	621	15,409
10-20%	2,569	2,649	1,880	1,230	1,010	9,337
10-15%	1,610	1,652	1,339	811	570	5,983
15-20%	959	997	541	418	439	3,355
20%-up	5,822	6,494	6,460	5,678	6,904	31,358
20-30%	2,282	2,235	1,876	1,466	1,141	8,999
30-40%	1,352	1,576	1,821	1,669	1,775	8,192
40-50%	790	976	883	900	1,310	4,859
50-75%	972	1,192	1,230	1,006	1,508	5,907
75%-up	427	516	651	638	1,170	3,401
Total	17,939	16,490	12,231	8,966	8,742	64,368

entirely or at least postpone entry into a nursing home.
Home equity conversion also can be seen as an alternative
income source for some of the elderly who need long-term
care services but are unable to finance long-term care
insurance during their retirement.[7]

Home equity represents the single largest asset for the
majority of elderly Americans. Approximately 12.5
million homes are owned by people 65 years of age and
older, and 80 percent of these homes have no outstanding

Table 4.2 *continued*

Percentage of Income	Age					Total
	65-69	70-74	75-79	80-84	85+	
Percentage Distribution						
0-5%	21	16	10	5	2	13
5-10%	33	28	22	18	7	24
10-20%	14	16	15	14	12	15
10-15%	9	10	11	9	7	9
15-20%	5	6	4	5	5	5
20%-up	33	39	53	63	79	49
20-30%	13	14	15	16	13	14
30-40%	8	10	15	19	20	13
40-50%	4	6	7	10	15	8
50-75%	5	7	10	11	17	9
75%-up	2	3	5	7	13	5
Total	100	100	100	100	100	100

Note: Calculations show the cost of the long-term care insurance (set at $2400 annually) as a percentage of *person-level* income. In other words, insurance is calculated as a percentage of family income for unmarried persons but as a percentage of only one-half of family income for married couples.

mortgages. The total equity of older home owners is estimated at $600 to $700 billion, and the average net equity holding is more than $60,000 per elderly household (Baldwin 1985). These assets become more striking when viewed as a proportion of the elderly person's life estate; home equity accounts for 70 percent of total assets held by elderly home owners and 83 percent of assets held by elderly single women (Jacobs 1985; Scholen 1985).

Traditionally, the accumulated equity in one's home remained illiquid and inaccessible as a source of cash until the property was sold. As a result, many elderly home owners with reduced retirement incomes find themselves in the untenable position of being "house rich but cash poor." The objective of home equity conversion is to unlock a home's value and to convert a portion of it into a steady stream of income without requiring the home owner to give up residency.

There are two main types of home equity conversion plans: reverse annuity mortgages (RAMs) and sale/leaseback mortgages. RAMs require the home owner to pledge some fraction of the home's equity to a lender in exchange for guaranteed monthly cash advances. The lump sum repayment of the principal and all accrued interest are deferred until the end of the loan term, when the home owner generally must sell the property to cover the loan balance.

This last feature of RAMs has been a source of controversy. Although in one sense it is fair and logical to have the owner sell the property at the end of the "reverse loan" period, it is an unpleasant occurrence. Bankers are reluctant to be in the unseemly position of appearing to "evict" an elderly home owner. To counter this criticism of RAMs, there is now some experimentation with reverse mortgages that guarantee home owners that they will never have to leave the home.

In sale/leaseback plans, the home owner sells the house, often at a discount, to another party in exchange for guaranteed life tenure in the home, an initial downpayment, and a steady stream of fully amortizing, fixed rate monthly payments. The amount of these payments depends on the term of the loan, which is determined by the joint and survivor life expectancy of the seller. The seller must make monthly rental payments back to the investor, and the buyer assumes responsibility for all property-related expenses.

Home equity conversion has some potential to lower government spending. Approximately 65 percent of America's elderly with incomes below the poverty line are home owners. More than 20 percent of the elderly poor, and about 30 percent of the near-poor elderly, have home equity in excess of $50,000 (Jacobs 1985; Jacobs and Weissert 1984). According to Jacobs (1985) one-quarter of all low-income elderly could raise their incomes above the poverty line by tapping the stored equity in their homes. But one must be careful not to consider this a panacea for the elderly. As shown in chapter 6, low-income status is more frequent among elderly persons who are renters than among home owners. Many of the frail elderly who are most at risk for long-term care services are renters, and that situation is not expected to change in the future.

SUPPORTIVE GOVERNMENT POLICIES

A wide range of policy options is available to encourage the spread of private long-term care insurance. Such policies include both the use of targeted subsidies and the favorable tax treatment of contributions made by employees and employers toward such insurance.

Some observers believe that the government could stimulate the demand for private long-term care insurance by creating some kind of a stop-loss program under Medicare. There are several ways to do this. First, the federal government could provide coverage after a specified waiting period (for example, two or three years). Such coverage would include a substantial copayment for covered services, which Medicaid would pay for the poor. The government could also provide subsidies for private insurance premiums for lower-income households that buy long-term care insurance to cover the waiting period.

An alternative approach involves a role for government as a reinsurer of private long-term care insurance policies. In this case, government coverage would kick in when a dollar threshold per case is triggered, as opposed to a time threshold. For example, the public coverage might start when a patient had incurred $50,000 of long-term care expenses.

Proponents of these approaches hope that the stop-loss protection will ease insurer fears about open-ended payouts and unlimited losses and that it would limit risk selection by insurers as they struggle to keep potential "outliers" out of their pool. Critics contend that these approaches would mainly benefit the relatively affluent elderly who could afford front-end private coverage and thereby protect their assets in full.

A third approach, developed by the author, involves introducing a set of refundable tax credits for out-of-pocket long-term care expenses that exceed a fixed proportion (e.g., 10 percent) of adjusted gross income. Everyone would be eligible for this credit, including those with no federal tax liability (this is why it is refundable).

Under this approach, households could count the full amount of a qualified long-term care insurance plan premium toward the 10 percent threshold. They could also count half of the expenses paid for out of pocket for long-term care, up to an annual maximum. Counting only a proportion of the expenses above the threshold and the use of a maximum are designed to put some cost control into the system. Counting premium payments in full would encourage people to purchase long-term care insurance.

The advantages of this approach are that it targets public aid to the relationship between long-term care expenses and income, which gets to the true nature of medical indigence; it fosters private insurance and conserves public resources; and it relates the amount that people pay to their ability to pay. The drawbacks include the difficulty of working out cash flow problems involved in a refundable tax credit approach and the difficulty of determining where to draw the line on eligible services, the payment of which should count toward the credit. This latter problem plagues virtually all long-term care financing arrangements.

Another approach involves a mandatory requirement that individuals set aside a certain amount of funds in an annuity during their working-age years that would be used to purchase long-term care insurance upon retirement (there would be a subsidy for this contribution for the unemployed and others with low incomes). This is a variation of the individual medical accounts approach. Such accounts, like IRAs, would receive preferential tax treatment; the proceeds could be withdrawn for use in meeting long-term care expenses without being subject to tax liability.

The federal government also could stimulate private long-term care insurance by conferring more favorable tax treatment on contributions made by employers and employees to the purchase of such insurance through work-based employee benefit packages.

Some states are beginning to develop long-term care financing packages. Some of these involve waiver of the spend-down requirements under Medicaid if a person has private long-term care insurance coverage. Others also add in subsidies for a portion of the premium, or deductibles and copayments, under such insurance. Thus, states are examining ways to regulate, promote, and subsidize long-term care insurance, or even to purchase it for those with low incomes.

Of course, some experts believe that all of these measures will fall short of providing the needed protection for tomorrow's elderly population. The recent Brookings study (Rivlin and Weiner 1988) advocates a two-tiered approach to financing long-term care in which a major new public social insurance program, funded by a payroll tax increase, would supplement the growth of private financing mechanisms.

Although there are important differences of opinion about the mix of public and private insurance for long-term care, most parties agree that we need to move from the current combination of out-of-pocket expenses and Medicaid to some form of an insurance-based approach that spreads risk across a broader base. Whether that base is all the elderly or the whole population is the subject of ongoing debate.

Increasing and Enhancing Personnel

A related concern that bears heavily on present and future long-term care capabilities is the health personnel shortage experienced nationwide. Nurses, aides, and therapists who do practice are increasingly drawn to positions with higher salaries than those typically offered in long-term care settings. Recruitment efforts need to focus on making long-term care opportunities more professionally attractive. Thus, solving labor bottleneck problems is one of the ingredients of a successful strategy of moving care toward the community setting.

In addition, the promotion of service approaches that use personnel with the greatest efficiency should help to ensure that essential services will not be precluded because of staffing constraints. The alternative models considered in this chapter do offer, as one of their benefits, this very opportunity to use available personnel resources more efficiently.

Notes, chapter four

1. This chapter was adapted from a longer paper by Jack A. Meyer, president, New Directions for Policy, and Ingrid M. Abolins, Economic and Social Research Institute.

2. Even though the main provisions of the Medicare Catastrophic Act were repealed in 1989, these provisions relating to Medicaid were retained.

3. This would be a fairly unrealistic scenario, because the cost of nursing home care has been increasing faster than the rate of inflation for the last 20 years (Holahan and Liu 1988, p. 8).

4. Tabulations from the August 1988 Current Population Survey.

5. The premiums do not increase with age but are set at initial purchase.

6. Some argue that the elderly need significant financial assets to protect before the purchase of LTC insurance makes sense, because they would quickly meet the Medicaid spend-down requirement (a house is a protected asset), should they need long-term care (Findlay 1989). In other words, they would spend more on the insurance over time than the value of their total financial assets. This argument ignores, however, the importance of protecting income and assets for a spouse and the freedom in the choice of care that accompanies private financing.

7. See chapter 6 for a discussion of the characteristics of the elderly who are expected to own homes in the future.

Chapter Five

MEETING THE SOCIAL SERVICES NEEDS OF THE ELDERLY

This chapter explores the future social services needs of the elderly.[1] The term "social services" generally refers to the needs of the frail elderly after their specific health and housing needs have been met. Services may include personal, financial, or nutrition services and are necessary to assist the frail elderly to reside in the community. Service providers may include family members, friends, community organizations, and paid service workers. Social services are a key element in the long-term care system--without this assistance many frail elderly persons would be forced to enter institutions.

The changing profile of the elderly should direct attention toward developing systems that deliver social services more broadly to the elderly population. Today, many disabled elderly receive no social services, and the vast majority of elderly who do receive help are assisted by family members (figure 5.1). Only about half of elderly persons with one or more limitations in activities of daily living (ADLs) received services in 1984, and, of those who received some help, 82 percent were assisted by family members, 32 percent received services from a non-relative, and 25 percent received some paid help.

This chapter explores the current delivery system to show how social services relate to the family, health, and income characteristics of the frail elderly population. It uses projection data to demonstrate that a continuation of current policies (including shrinking government resources devoted to social services and a lack of incentives to encourage a broader private service delivery market) will have disastrous effects in the future. There will be many more frail elderly, and a smaller proportion of them will have family members available to provide social service support. Thus, more effective delivery of social services will be required to dampen the demand for more expensive institutional care arrangements, and at the same time to serve the elderly's desire to live independently. The elderly will need a more generous and supportive system in which health, housing and social services needs are handled in an integrated fashion.

HOW DOES THE CURRENT SYSTEM WORK?

It is both informative and distressing when one tries to describe how the current "system" works. One almost always begins not with what people need but with which fund will pay for specific types of care (and which care for which people will not be covered). The reason behind this pattern is that most social service needs for most people in the United States are *not* provided through government efforts or private insurance. Analogous to the current long-term care system, many elderly people with social service needs cannot get services without exhausting their own and their families' resources.

What are the potential social services needs of the elderly? *Social services* is not a very carefully defined term. It generally refers to services that enable an individual to continue to maintain residence in the community in the least restrictive setting possible and to provide support

Figure 5.1   Use of Social Services
by the Disabled Elderly
Living in the Community, 1984

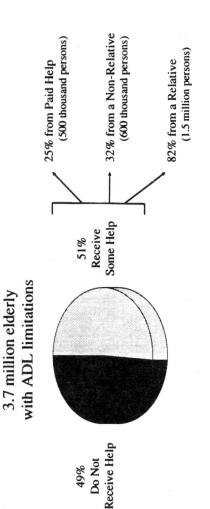

3.7 million elderly
with ADL limitations

49%
Do Not
Receive Help

51%
Receive
Some Help

25% from Paid Help
(500 thousand persons)

32% from a Non-Relative
(600 thousand persons)

82% from a Relative
(1.5 million persons)

Source: The 1984 Supplement on Aging

and assistance to family or other care givers. Social services may include the following:

- *Homemaker/chore services.* These include grocery shopping, yard work, house cleaning, laundry, meal preparation, and other specific tasks and chores).

- *Personal care.* This would include bathing, dressing, and so on.

- *Financial services.* Such services include managing a person's money, paying bills, or being a representative payee for government benefits.

- *Out-of-home day care.* This includes social adult day care, often accompanied by nutrition and health services.

- *Out-of-home respite care.* Usually, such care is overnight care, for a few days at most, to give usual care givers a rest and some time to themselves or to enable them to take necessary business trips, and so on.

- *Protective services.* These are for adults in immediate danger of death or serious harm to themselves, who cannot help themselves and who have no one else to help them; can include legal, housing, guardianship, financial, medical, social, competency, and other concerns.

- *Casework.* This, essentially, is helping people get the benefits and services they need and are eligible for.

- *Counseling.* Counseling may include individual or group counseling to help the person and his or her family and other care givers to adjust to the changed needs of the elderly person.

- *Miscellaneous.* Such services include transportation and the social aspect of congregate meals.

Defining a "need" for social services is even more difficult than defining the parameters of the services themselves. Because social services for the elderly are intended to facilitate continued independent residence in the community and to prevent or delay institutionalization, "need" has usually been related to some observable measure of limitation in activities considered essential for daily life outside of institutions. Two related concepts are Activities of Daily Living (ADLs) and Instrumental Activities of Daily Living (IADLs). ADLs include dressing, eating, toileting, mobility, and bathing. IADLs include shopping, using the telephone, doing heavy and light housework, preparing meals, and managing money. ADLs represent more severe limitations than IADLs, but inability to perform several IADLs may seriously constrain a person's ability to live independently even if the person has no ADL limitations. A care giver living with someone with several IADL limitations will experience some increased responsibilities but is not likely to find these as restrictive or demanding as the responsibilities that fall on a care giver to someone who has several ADL limitations.

It is relatively easy to maintain, as a rule of thumb, that a person with no ADL or IADL limitations has no need for social services, whether that person is living alone or with other people. It might also be readily agreed that a person with several ADL and several IADL limitations clearly does need social services, even if there is a live-in care giver. The definitional problem arises in the less clear-cut cases: for example, a person with only one or two IADL limitations living alone, or a person with two IADL and one ADL limitation and living with a care giver. Further complicating the picture of need is the fact that many older people make do without assistance even when they have demonstrable need. As will be seen below, many older people who need help to perform ADLs or IADLs do not get it. Their ability to lead full lives may be considerably restricted as a result, even when they manage to remain outside of institutions.

The amount of "need" for social services among the elderly will vary in direct relation to the level of disability that policymakers accept as a criterion. For reference, many existing programs use the presence of one ADL limitation as their criterion of need (Struyk et al. 1988). Using this criterion, 1 of every 7 persons over age 65 living in their communities in the United States in 1984 needed social services.[2] Using the criterion of two or more ADL limitations, 1 of every 12 elderly people needed social services. Yet only about 1 in 20 received such help in 1984.

WHO AND WHAT ARE COVERED BY PRESENT FEDERAL PROGRAMS?

Only three federal programs routinely cover social services. The three programs are the Social Services Block Grant (SSBG),[3] the Older Americans Act (OAA), and Medicaid (under state options and waivers). The two largest of these, the SSBG and Medicaid, are available only to the very poor who meet the programs' stringent income and assets eligibility criteria (and in the case of Medicaid, level of disability criteria as well).

The Social Services Block Grant

Most services funded through the SSBG are means-tested, and, in general, only people whose incomes are less than 115 percent of the federal poverty level are eligible.[4] Social services for the elderly under the SSBG come under the program goal of "preventing or reducing inappropriate institutional care by providing for community-based care, home-based care, or other forms of less intensive care." Special provision is made under the SSBG for protective services. Elderly persons (as well as the nonelderly) who are in circumstances that present an immediate danger to their life or safety are entitled to protective services without regard to income.

Funding for the entire SSBG program was $2.7 billion in 1987--a figure that represents a 36 percent reduction from the purchasing power of funding available through Title XX in 1980. The reduction was a combination of the cuts enacted in 1981, when Title XX was converted into the SSBG, and losses caused by failure to keep up with inflation.

Moreover, only a small part of these monies are used to support services for the elderly. Gaberlavage (1987) reports that 47 states currently use some of their SSBG allocation to provide social services to the elderly, including homemaker, chore, companionship, and home maintenance services. Among these 47 states, the proportion of SSBG funds spent on elderly services ranged from 1 to 50 percent, with an average of 18 percent ($486 million, nationwide). In the scramble that resulted from federal changes and cuts under the Omnibus Budget Reconciliation Act of 1981, which transformed Title XX into the SSBG, many states shifted their SSBG funding patterns to protect children's services at the expense of services for the elderly (Burt and Pittman 1985). In recent years the shrinkage in SSBG purchasing power caused by the federal funding cap (at $2.7 billion annually since 1984) and the effects of inflation will probably mean decreased funding for services for the elderly that are used to maintain independence or prevent institutionalization, in relation to mandated protective services (Struyk et al. 1988, p. 62).

The Older Americans Act

The Older Americans Act (OAA) contains provisions "intended to assist older persons to attain maximum independence in a home environment, to remove individual and social barriers to economic and personal independence, and to provide services and care for the vulnerable elderly" (Special Committee on Aging, U.S. Senate 1986 p. 338).

The OAA's major contribution to the well-being of the elderly (measured in terms of money) is nutritional. Approximately 67 percent of the OAA's annual appropriation (or $559 million in 1987) is devoted to congregate meals (42 percent), home-delivered meals (9 percent), and USDA commodities (17 percent). Of the remaining $270 million (in fiscal year 1987), probably less than half is used for social services, including homemaker and home health aide services. The Administration on Aging (AOA) does not have breakdowns of funding for separate supportive services. User service statistics indicate, however, that only about 17 percent of the users of AOA supportive services used the core social services of homemaker, home health aide and outreach/protective services.[5]

OAA services are available to all elderly individuals, regardless of income. Even though older people with the greatest social or economic needs are supposed to receive priority, no means testing is allowed that would assure appropriate targeting. This would not be a problem if the

OAA had sufficient resources to serve all those who needed social services, but in fact the Older Americans Act does not provide anywhere near the necessary level of funding. Using the presence of one or more ADL limitations as a rough estimate of need for social services, in 1987 OAA homemaker/home health aide services could have reached only 14 percent of the almost 6 million older Americans with one or more ADL limitations.[6]

Medicaid

There are several options for funding home health, homemaker, and personal care services through Medicaid, all of which have serious limitations in meeting the need for social services to maintain independent living situations for older persons. Under Medicaid, such services must be tied either to a medical need and ordered by a physician (optional state coverage under a Medicaid state plan), or be used to prevent institutionalization for people who are nursing-home certifiable (two waiver programs). Under the waiver programs the provision of home-based services either must be cost-neutral (Home and Community Based Waiver--section 2176) or must be accompanied by a state cap on total Medicaid spending for long-term care (combining funding for home-based services and nursing home services--section 4102 waiver). Fiscal year 1986 funding under the first two of these programs totaled $1.4 million (Struyk et al. 1988, p. 68); the third option (Section 4102) was created in late 1987, and cost data are not available.

Under any of the Medicaid options, in addition to "medically oriented" restrictions, a person must be eligible for Medicaid before being able to receive supportive social services. Medicaid eligibility is a problem for many old people with substantial needs for social services. Historically, Medicaid eligibility for the elderly who need social services delivered in the community has been tied to eligibility for or receipt of SSI, a means-tested income support program for the elderly and disabled. The Medicare Catastrophic Act of 1988, however, requires that the states phase in coverage for all elderly below the poverty line by 1992. There will still be barriers to entry, however, because of asset tests and the detailed applications process. Indeed, recent research shows that the Medicaid participation rate is quite low for elderly persons who are eligible for Medicaid but are not receiving Supplemental Security Income (SSI) or living in institutions.[7] The expansion of Medicaid coverage to the elderly poor is not likely to change this situation.

In addition to the inadequacy of funding levels for social services in federal programs, gaining access to the resources that do exist is also often a problem for the elderly. Medicaid eligibility usually is determined by the income maintenance unit of a health and welfare agency. Services funded by the SSBG may be accessed through the social services unit of the same agency that administers Medicaid, but through a separate application and eligibility determination process. However, SSBG services usually are provided by nonprofit agencies, and potential clients frequently must go directly to those agencies to apply. Older Americans Act funds are administered through yet another bureaucracy, the Area Agencies on Aging. Some Area Agencies maintain centralized application procedures, but OAA social services access may also be administered directly by the nonprofits that provide the service. This welter of offices and application processes that must be negotiated to obtain social services definitely poses a barrier to access to services.

WHICH PEOPLE AND SERVICES ARE NOT
COVERED BY PRESENT PROGRAMS?

There is no single, universally accepted definition of "need" for social services. However, a commonly used operational definition of need is that a person has at least one limitation in Activities of Daily Living (eating, bathing, toileting, dressing, mobility). As table 5.1 shows, of the 26.4 million people over age 65 in the United States in 1984, 14 percent, or 3.7 million people, reported at least one ADL limitation. Of these, more than half (or 2 million people) have two or more ADL limitations.[8]

Using data from the 1984 Supplement on Aging (a supplement to the National Health Interview Survey), it is possible to summarize people's reported use of *formal* in-home social/health services that might assist someone with ADL limitations to remain in the community.[9] The services assessed were home-delivered meals, homemaker services, visiting nurse services, home health aide, and adult day care. The most striking finding is that only 6 percent of the elderly reported using some in-home services (table 5.2), even though 14 percent have one or more ADLs. The use (or lack of use) of social services varies by household composition. Those who live alone and those who live without a spouse but with their adult child are more likely to use services than those who live with a spouse. But no more than 10 percent of the elderly in any category of household composition report using any in-home services. The fact that only 30 percent of elderly persons who live alone and have three or more ADL limitations received in-home services illustrates dramatically the extent of the service gap (table 5.2).

Table 5.1   PERCENTAGE OF COMMUNITY-BASED
ELDERLY POPULATION IN 1984 WITH ADL
AND IADL LIMITATIONS, BY AGE (weighted
percentages)

Percentage	65-74	75-84	85+	Total
By number of ADL limitations[a]				
0	90	83	65	86
1	5	8	13	7
2	2	3	9	3
3	1	3	5	2
4	1	2	5	2
5	1	1	3	1
Total percentage	100.0	100.0	100.0	100.0
Number of persons (000)	16.3	8.2	1.9	26.4
By number of IADL limitations[b]				
0	79	66	44	72
1	13	17	15	14
2	2	6	9	4
3	2	3	8	3
4	2	4	8	3
5	1	2	7	2
6	1	2	9	2
Total percentage	100.0	100.0	100.0	100.0
Number of persons (000)	16.3	8.2	1.9	26.4

Source: 1984 Supplement on Aging, National Health Interview Survey.

a.   ADLs are measured by Katz scale: bathing, dressing, eating, transferring, and toileting (see text, chapter 2).

b.   IADLs measured are preparing meals, shopping, managing money, telephoning, heavy housework, and light housework.

Table 5.2 USE OF FORMAL SOCIAL SERVICES IN 1984 BY
ADL LIMITATIONS AND LIVING CIRCUMSTANCE

Number of ADL Limitations	Total	Alone	With Spouse	With Child	With Others
	Thousands of Persons Who Use Some Services				
0	717	378	222	65	54
1	247	149	47	29	23
2	146	69	45	18	14
3 or more	508	95	155	102	36
Total	1,618	691	469	214	127
	Percentage of All Elderly Persons Who Use Some Social Services				
0	3.2	5.3	2.0	4.0	3.0
1	14.4	20.5	7.8	12.9	13.3
2	17.7	26.1	12.4	15.1	17.2
3 or more	32.9	30.0	32.5	37.0	28.0
Total	6.0	8.2	6.0	9.5	5.8
	All Elderly (thousands of persons)				
0	22,693	7,092	12,160	1,628	1,813
1	1,720	731	591	226	172
2	829	265	360	121	83
3 or more	1,191	310	476	276	129
Total	26,433	8,398	13,587	2,251	2,197

Source: 1984 Supplement on Aging, National Health Interview Survey.

Note: Social services include home-delivered meals, homemaker services, visiting nurse service, home health aide, and adult day care.

Of course, limitations in ADLs are heavily associated with age, such that fewer than 1 in 10 individuals age 65 to 74 have one or more ADL limitations, compared to about 1 in 6 for those age 75 to 84 and about 1 in 3 for those 85 or older (table 5.1). Limitations in IADLs are similarly associated with age: 1 in 4 people age 65 to 74 had one or more IADL limitations in 1984, as did 1 in 3 of those age 75 to 84, and about 3 in 5 of those 85 or older.

The more ADL or IADL limitations, the more likely that older persons report use of at least one in-home social/ health service. Nevertheless, such services do not reach a great many persons with relatively severe disabilities; for example, just 32.9 percent (508,000 people) of those with three or more ADL limitations receive any in-home services, leaving 807,498 elderly persons with three or more ADL limitations with no formal, in-home services.

The presence in the home of one or more individuals who might care for an elderly person with many ADL limitations certainly would reduce the need for formal services. But of the 1.2 million older people with three or more ADL limitations, 1 of 4 live alone (310,000 people), and only 30 percent of these receive any in-home services (table 5.2). It is also true that the segment of the elderly population that lives with a child but without a spouse (2.3 million people) is *most* likely to report the receipt of in-home services at ages 65 to 84. Moreover, data on service utilization by age (not shown in table 5.2) indicate that at age 85 and above, those living alone are most likely to get services. At every age, the group of the elderly living with a child but without a spouse has more ADL and IADL limitations than the general elderly population. This appears to be a major reason for their higher use of services, even with the presence of a live-in family care giver.

Many older people with limitations in ADLs and IADLs report that although they need help, they do not get any.

Table 5.3 presents data on need for and receipt of assistance for the elderly population 65 and older in 1984. Depending on the ADL limitation, 29 to 64 percent of those who need help do not get it (second column of table 5.3). Of the elderly who do get some help for ADLs that they have difficulty performing, the greatest amount of this assistance is unpaid (72 to 80 percent) and comes from relatives (76 to 86 percent). Relatively few people receive help from nonrelatives (18 to 33 percent, depending on the ADL limitation). People are most likely to receive paid help for bathing, eating, and toileting and are least likely to receive paid help for dressing and transferring.

A higher proportion of the elderly with IADL limitations report getting help than do the elderly with the more severe ADL health limitations. Most of the help comes from relatives. Some 26 percent of the elderly report that they have some difficulty with one or more IADLs (table 5.3). Between 2 and 36 percent of those who need help do not get it, depending on the IADL limitation. Of those who do get help, the proportion who pay for any help ranges from 8 to 30 percent, and the proportion who get any help from nonrelatives ranges from 10 to 31 percent. Relatives supply assistance in 72 to 94 percent of the cases. Older people are most likely to purchase housework and prepared meals and are least likely to pay someone to manage their money for them.

One question that arises is whether social services are going to poor people who qualify for public benefits or whether the few who are getting services are those who can afford to pay for them. The relationship of social services receipt to poverty is complex. Data already reported indicate that receipt of services is more likely at higher levels of ADL limitations. It is also true that the presence of ADL limitations is associated with higher proportions of older people living in households below the poverty threshold. Only 12 percent of those with no ADL

Table 5.3   PROPORTION OF ELDERLY POPULATION IN
1984 WITH ADL AND IADL LIMITATIONS WHO
GET HELP, AND SOURCE OF HELP

Limitation	Have Difficulty	Percentage of Those Who Have Difficulty	
	% of 65+ Population	Get No Help	Get Help
ADL Limitation			
Bathing	10	39	61
Dressing	6	29	71
Eating	2	39	61
Transferring	8	64	36
Toileting	4	47	53
One or more ADLs	14[a]	49	51
IADL Limitation			
Meals	7	15	85
Shopping	12	8	92
Money management	5	2	98
Phoning	5	36	64
Heavy housework	26	18	82
Light housework	7	12	88
One or more IADLs	26[a]	15	85

Source: 1984 Supplement on Aging, National Health Interview Survey.

Limitation	Percentage of Those Who Get Help[b]		
	% Getting Any Help From a Nonrelative	% Getting Help From Relatives	% Paying For Any Help
ADL Limitation			
Bathing	33	76	28
Dressing	30	84	20
Eating	18	80	27
Transferring	24	86	21
Toileting	26	87	26
One or more ADLs	32	82	25
IADL Limitation			
Meals	27	82	24
Shopping	23	85	14
Money management	10	94	8
Phoning	13	89	13
Heavy housework	25	72	30
Light housework	31	77	26
One or more IADLs	37	80	32

a. Differs from earlier estimates because missing data on one or more variables involved in calculating these figures.

b. Persons may get help from several sources.

Table 5.4   PERCENTAGE OF ELDERLY WITH ADLs
RECEIVING AT LEAST ONE SOCIAL SERVICE,
BY POVERTY STATUS IN 1984

Household Income	Number of Limitations in Activities of Daily Living (ADLS)					
	0	1	2	3	4	5
Above poverty	3	12	14	24	27	49
Below poverty	6	18	33	34	39	46
Unknown	3	17	16	25	38	38

Source: 1984 Supplement on Aging, National Health Interview Study.

limitations live in poverty, 21 percent of those with one
ADL limitation live in poverty, and 17 to 20 percent of
those with two or more ADL limitations live in poverty.
This association of poverty and limitations in ADLs is
confounded by age, because both poverty and the incidence of ADL limitations increase with age among the
elderly.

Service receipt levels and increases in services at higher
levels of ADL limitations are curvilinearly related to a
household's poverty status (table 5.4). At none or one
ADL limitation, only 3 to 6 percentage points separate the
proportion of households above and below the threshold
that receive services. But at levels of two to four ADL
limitations, 10 to 19 percent more poor households receive
services than households above the poverty level. The
proportion below the threshold is more likely to receive
services at every level of ADL limitations except for
persons with five or more ADL limitations. This distribution suggests that government programs for the very poor
are making social services available to those who need

them at the same or higher rates as those above the poverty threshold are able to obtain them. *Nevertheless, even at very high levels of four or more ADL limitations, no more than half of the elderly households, poor or not, receive these services.*

In summary, it is obvious that the vast majority (94 percent) of the elderly do not receive any social services. Even many of those with severe needs for social services-- those with ADL limitations and no significant live-in caretakers in their lives--do not receive these services under the present system.

PROBLEMS WITH THE CURRENT SYSTEM

The current system of social services for the elderly has many problems. Several are interrelated: that the system is designed to be excessively concerned with which program will pay for specific services; that it is too compartmentalized into health, housing, social services, mental health, and other services as separate delivery systems; and that it is too inflexible to meet the needs of individuals, which may shift substantially within relatively short periods. In addition to the system's inability to serve the needs of many elderly persons, it offers little or no support to the individuals--usually family members--who provide the great bulk of the care received by the frail elderly. Finally, a very serious problem is the system's failure to cover many people who cannot afford to purchase the care they need on the private market.

From every side one repeatedly hears that certain services are or are not available because a particular program will or will not pay for them. Case managers, after assessing a client's service needs, often cannot focus on obtaining the best mix of services but first must address the issue of client eligibility for different funding sources and then select the services for which the funding source will pay. If the client is not eligible for any public funding source, the case manager often has no alternatives to recommend. This circumstance results in both overservice and underservice.

Overservice occurs, for example, when someone needs some types of service but does not need a medical level of care. Yet the person qualifies for Medicaid, which will pay for a higher level of care than needed, and there is no other source of potential funding for a lesser level of care. In a similar manner, placement in nursing homes frequently occurs when there is no financial resource available to pay for in-home social and health services, even though the client does not need 24-hour medical care.

Underservice occurs when there is no source of funding for services that would meet an older person's needs. If individuals or their families cannot afford to purchase the care themselves, the need goes unmet or only partially met. The data presented above, on the numbers of elderly who have difficulty with certain activities but receive no help in performing them, document the level of unmet need.

The current system's compartmentalization and accompanying failure to meet the needs of the elderly can be seen at many turns. Perhaps the most dramatic is the situation routinely encountered by adult protective services workers.[10] Adult protective services come into play when persons pose an immediate threat to their own life or safety, cannot take care of their own needs, and have no one else who can provide appropriate care. The group of people requiring adult protective services contains a very large proportion of elderly individuals.

Adult protective services cases usually begin with an emergency. Often the only agency in town with emergen-

cy response capability that includes picking up and holding a person for his or her own safety is the mental health
system. In many jurisdictions the mental health and social
services systems are not coordinated, and mental health
can refuse to assist in an emergency for anyone who is not
already a mental health client. Housing with supportive
services is often a pressing need that cannot be met
because it is completely unavailable, because of its cost, or
because of the separation of the systems that control each
type of assistance, even if leaving clients in their present
circumstances is dangerous to them. Mental competency
to handle one's own affairs is often an issue that takes time
to resolve through legal means, yet timely receipt of
needed services in the interim often is difficult to arrange.
Because adult protective services under the SSBG is the one
social service that can be offered independent of income,
clients sometimes do not qualify for the means-tested
social services that might help them remain in independent or semi-independent circumstances. In short, the
complex emergency situations usually faced by adult
protective services highlight the failures of coordination
among current sources of social and other services.

Another indication of the same system failures comes
from a recent review of social services delivery to the
elderly in assisted housing (Struyk et al. 1988). Approximately 1.5 million elderly renters live in assisted housing.
Of these, about 7 percent require assistance to perform one
or more ADLs. This study indicates that the most efficient
and effective arrangement for delivering social services,
currently being practiced in a number of states, is to
provide the housing manager with a fixed amount to
spend per person. The housing manager then can hire
someone to coordinate services and can either hire personnel to provide the services or can arrange contracted
services. From the older person's point of view, all
contacts to obtain services occur at the place of residence.

This approach appears more efficient than one that asks a case manager to help elderly clients negotiate separate eligibility procedures in several off-site agencies to obtain needed services, and then probably forces them to deal with more than one person coming into their homes to deliver those services.

Elderly people with activity limitations or disabilities who might benefit from social services often would be most assisted by flexible arrangements that mostly are not possible at present. Flexibility of service delivery ideally would be used to reduce or eliminate the need to change residences to obtain services. Such moves are very disruptive for older people. They often mean leaving behind connections to a neighborhood in which the person is known, as well as leaving a home. These changes can have serious effects on identity and self-esteem, which in turn can affect adjustment and even longevity in the new environment. There also is some evidence that people resist moves that have clear connotations of decreasing abilities, such as a move into a facility identified with residents who require increased levels of care. The more a person sees these moves as permanent and irreversible, the greater their impact.

The present system of care, with its relative lack of available social services even for people with severe levels of disability, unduly ties levels of care to specific residence options. If you want the care, you must move to where you can get it--usually a nursing home. Even in assisted housing developments for the elderly, only recently has there been experimentation on a very small scale with providing social services to extend the viable length of stay of residents. The general rule is that one must be completely independent in ADLs and IADLs to live in a senior high rise (although the reality is often that people need help, but simply do not get it). Many senior assisted housing complexes serve as sites for congregate meals, and many have social directors who plan for visits from county nurses for blood pressure and podiatry checkups. But it is the rare senior housing complex that makes the full range of social services available to its residents so that those with several ADL or IADL limitations can receive the help needed to remain in their homes. Evidence from recent state innovations (Struyk et al. 1988) strongly suggests that it is possible to deliver social services at reasonable cost and with reasonable targeting to assist those most in need.

Another aspect of flexibility that is frequently lacking in the present system is the ability to return to one's home after a hospitalization and possible subsequent nursing home stay. Because a person's activity limitations or disabilities may increase as a consequence of the condition that led to hospitalization, he or she may no longer be able to maintain a completely independent lifestyle yet also may not need 24-hour care. At present there are not enough social services, with enough flexibility, to help many people return to their own homes. The situation is compounded when the elderly person is renting, either from a private landlord or in assisted housing. Here the issue becomes how long a landlord will hold an apartment. Because assisted housing often has very long waiting lists, this can be an issue even when the rent is paid. It is all the more intimidating to older people to seek medical care they may need if they fear losing their housing as a result. The practice of holding apartments for relatively short periods thus may turn a potentially reversible trip to the hospital or nursing home into a permanent one.

The final difficulty with the present system is its almost complete inability to serve the needs of the "not absolutely poor." To be eligible for Medicaid one must be absolutely poor. The social services funded under the SSBG are somewhat more flexible and, at the discretion of the states, may serve households at up to 115 percent of the poverty level. The programs of the Older Americans Act are the only ones not means-tested, but there is relatively little money in these programs and they serve a relatively high proportion of poor people.

Virtually no private insurance policies cover ongoing social services (a few may cover selected social services for short periods when ordered by a physician in conjunction with an immediately prior hospital stay). Thus, people with little discretionary money, but too much money to qualify for the means-tested programs, cannot afford to purchase social services for themselves. The system contains a large gap between the few among the very poor who are lucky enough to get the limited government-supported services, and the relatively rich who can afford to pay for private services. The vast majority of the elderly with social services needs fall in between and are lost in the cracks of the "system."

In summary, today's elderly sometimes go without needed assistance that social services could provide. The care they do get is overwhelmingly supplied free by relatives, most of whom live with the person receiving care. To meet the need for services and to prevent both "doing without" and unnecessary institutionalization, we need to create a system with the following characteristics:

- All people who cannot afford to purchase needed care can obtain it through government or private insurance mechanisms.

- Social services are available independent of residence--people living in their own homes, in senior high rises, in residential communities, or in group accommodations could all receive the services they need.

- Both private insurance and government insurance or other programs cover necessary social services to people residing in the community.

- Support and assistance are available to family care givers to prevent "burnout" and enable them to continue giving their family members the care they need.

- Funding is flexible enough to cover what people need, whether it is housing, transportation, personal care, home maintenance, chore service, medical care, or money management.

FUTURE SERVICE NEEDS

The factors that will require a more coherent system of social and other services are clear. There will be far more elderly persons with social service requirements in the future. As discussed earlier, the elderly population is expected to double at least between 1990 and 2030, and the proportion of elderly with some health limitations is expected to increase at a faster rate. In addition, more elderly persons will be living alone and will have to depend on formal in-home services.

As presented earlier, more than one-third of the elderly population is expected to have some health limitation in 2010 and in 2030. Figure 5.2 outlines the dimensions of potential need for services. In 1990 there will be 9.2 million elderly persons with either limitations in ADLs or in IADLs. Twenty years later, in 2010, there are expected to be 12 to 13 million elderly with health limitations, and in 2030 the number will reach 19 to 22 million elderly persons. Contrast these numbers to the number of persons who receive some formal services today. In 1984 only 1.6 million elderly persons living in the community reported

Table 5.5   FUTURE ELDERLY LIVING IN THE COMMUNITY, BY DEGREE OF DISABILITY

	1990	2010			2030		
		Base-Case	Optimistic Mortality	Optimistic Mortality & Health	Base-Case	Optimistic Mortality	Optimistic Mortality & Health
		Millions of Persons					
No ADL or IADL limitations	21.1	26.0	27.8	28.6	40.9	45.1	47.3
IADL limitations only	4.6	6.0	6.6	6.9	9.4	10.7	11.4
1 IADL limitation	3.3	4.2	4.5	4.7	6.6	7.4	7.8
2 IADL limitations	.7	1.0	1.1	1.1	1.5	1.7	1.8
3 or more IADL limitations	.6	.9	1.0	1.1	1.3	1.6	1.7
ADL limitations	4.6	6.2	6.7	6.0	9.8	11.4	9.5
1 ADL limitation	2.0	2.8	2.9	2.4	4.2	4.7	3.7
2 ADL limitations	1.1	1.5	1.7	1.6	2.3	2.7	2.3
3 or more ADL limitations	1.5	2.0	2.2	2.0	3.2	4.0	3.5
Total	30.3	38.2	41.1	41.5	60.1	67.2	68.2

		2010			2030		
	1990	Base-Case	Optimistic Mortality	Optimistic Mortality & Health	Base-Case	Optimistic Mortality	Optimistic Mortality & Health
				Percentage Distribution			
No ADL or IADL limitations	70	68	68	69	68	67	69
IADL limitations only	15	16	16	17	16	16	17
1 IADL limitation	11	11	11	11	11	11	12
2 IADL limitations	2	3	3	3	2	3	3
3 or more IADL limitations	2	2	3	3	2	2	3
ADL limitations	15	16	16	14	16	17	14
1 ADL limitation	7	7	7	6	7	7	5
2 ADL limitations	4	4	4	4	4	4	3
3 or more ADL limitations	5	5	5	5	5	6	5
Total	100	100	100	100	100	100	100

Figure 5.2   **Potential Need for Social Services**

Persons Over Age 65
Living in the Community, 1990-2030

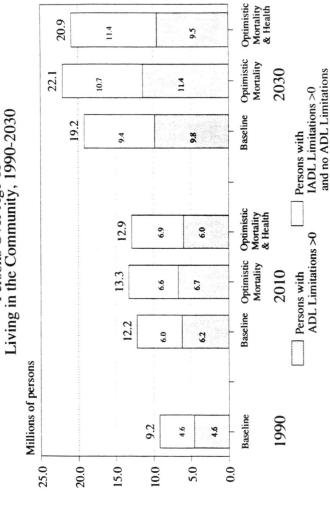

Source: Projections of The Urban Institute's DYNASIM model

receiving some formal care. Moreover, the gap in care giving (the number of elderly wanting care minus those who actually received care) estimated for 1984 was already significant.

Table 5.5 shows the expected degree of disability of the future elderly living in the community under the three mortality/health scenarios projected. Using a social services need criterion of two or more IADL limitations or at least one ADL limitation, 5.9 million elderly persons could benefit from social services in 1990. This represents 19.6 percent of the community-based elderly population. This number is expected to rise to between 8.1 and 8.8 million persons by 2010 and to between 12.6 and 14.7 million persons by 2030. As shown, the estimated "rate of need" rises slightly after 1990 as the population ages, except under the optimistic health scenario, which predicts a declining rate of need.

OPTIONS FOR TYPES OF SERVICES

Social services are facilitative; they help people maintain a maximum degree of independence, assure that they receive the benefits to which they are entitled, connect people with needed services, and perform other enabling activities. Social services work best when contact is easy, both for people to seek out the social worker and for the social worker to visit with them. The facilitative nature of social services has some clear implications for how services should be set up.

Ideally, social services for the elderly would be integrated with housing, nutrition and health services, and enrichment activities (such as education and personal growth) both physically and financially. Certain retirement communities today (usually, life care communities, in which one invests one's assets in exchange for assured care and support) exhibit this type of integration. Housing options in such communities often range from single-family detached homes; to apartments; to housing with housekeeping, meals, and some personal care services; to skilled nursing and hospital facilities. Individuals remain in the same community but move between housing options as needed for their health and level of functioning. Movement is not entirely one-way (toward ever-increasing levels of care). Rather, someone can go from an apartment to the hospital, then to a skilled nursing facility, and then back to his or her apartment, with support services as needed.

One of the drawbacks of life care communities is that many elderly people do not like the idea of moving into "the place they are going to die." Its finality (augmented by turning over all of one's assets) is perceived as too depressing, as not leaving enough room for surprises, flexibility, new directions. Another serious drawback is that many older people do not have the resources to invest in such communities.

The same flexibility and comprehensiveness exhibited by life care communities also has been built into a few care systems that are not physically part of the same community corporation, and that are not entirely self-pay. For example, in one city older people may live in their own apartment in a senior high rise (Section 202 supported) that also houses a Senior Center and social services offices for county social workers and serves one congregate meal a day. Across the street is another apartment complex for seniors, which has two floors of apartments devoted to individuals or couples who need some personal care and some assistance with shopping, cleaning, or money management. These people receive two congregate meals every day. Contracts exist with nursing homes and hospitals in this city to treat residents as they need it. Social workers coordinate movement between senior housing and medical facilities; residents' apartments are maintained for them so that they may return from hospital or nursing home stays when they are well enough.

To the maximum extent possible, an ideal social services system would provide coverage for all people who meet established criteria of need. The system would deliver the services in people's homes, whether those homes were in congregate settings (for example, senior high rises) or in individual dwelling units scattered around a community. Older people needing social services would be able to maintain maximum continuity with neighborhood and community that offer them rootedness and identity, and to which they have a sense of contributing as well as receiving. An ideal system would pay attention to older people's need for continued stimulation and growth, as well as to their need for health and personal care and housekeeping.

Such a system would make available a full continuum of housing options, with assistance as needed to make and keep them affordable. Greater help in achieving a variety of shared housing options will be needed, and ideally these will foster interdependence, with coresidents exchanging services and supportive activities within the scope of their abilities. Sliding-scale copayments for social services and regular assessments by social services managers will help to assure that services are not overused.

An absolutely essential feature of an ideal system is flexibility. It cannot compartmentalize its benefits if it is to respond adequately to individual needs. Ideally, it might work as a sort of capitation system, in which the system manager (for example, a case manager for people living in their own homes, or a housing manager for people living in congregate settings) had available a certain quantity of resources that, on average, could be expended on individual system users. Some people might require more services than others, but, on average, outlays would balance. The manager could broker available services, could purchase frequently used services and benefit from economies of scale, could tailor service packages as needed. The key to success of such systems would be their ability to span the range of needed services, including health, mental health, housing, social services, transportation, income maintenance, and legal services. Regular contacts and consultations with individuals would indicate what services were needed and wanted; the manager then would arrange for these to be delivered.

An ideal system also would foster a maximum amount of interdependence. It will be important not to infantilize older people, treating them as if they now have nothing to contribute and are fated simply to absorb resources and the efforts of others. Elderly individuals with complementary abilities could assist each other in necessary activities. Every effort should be made to maintain involvement in community activities in whatever ways each individual continues to be able to function.

As the ratio of older people to younger family members and to the younger population in general increases, the question arises of who will provide the services needed by the elderly. Live-in relatives, who now give the bulk of assistance, virtually all unpaid, will be in shorter supply. Greater interdependence among neighbors will need to be fostered, as will innovative shared housing arrangements. Capitated or other social insurance schemes will be needed to support equitable availability of social services, and a substantial amount of public investment in these schemes probably will be necessary. Finally, the social service needs of the elderly in 2030 are likely to entail a substantial demand on trained personnel who can coordinate and deliver in-home services, because even with every effort to increase community and mutual support among nonrelatives, the ability of informal care givers to meet the need is likely to be substantially less than it is now.

Notes, chapter five

1. This chapter was written by Martha Burt, who is currently a senior fellow at the Russel Sage Foundation.

2. An ADL limitation is defined as "have difficulty with" an activity of daily living rather than the more restrictive definition of "requires assistance with" (tabulations from the 1984 Supplement on Aging to the National Health Interview Survey; see chapter 2 for a full discussion of these results).

3. Previously, this was Title XX of the Social Security Act.

4. There is some variation in eligibility by state since the SSBG took over, with the result that recipients are probably poorer, on average.

5. Figures supplied by Administration on Aging, DHHS, Joanne Moore, personal communication, 1989.

6. Author's calculation from unpublished service statistics for 1987 and estimated number of elderly with ADL limitations.

7. Based on an Urban Institute analysis of the characteristics of the Medicaid-eligible population compared with the Medicaid-enrollee population in the March 1988 Current Population Survey (unpublished tabulations).

8. These figures only refer to the elderly living in their communities. See chapter 2 for figures on ADLs for the total elderly population, including both those in institutions and those residing in the community. ADLs were measured using the Katz scale, a relatively conservative measure of impairment, which assesses limitations in five activities: dressing, eating, bathing,

toileting, and transferring (for example, getting out of bed). As noted in chapter 2, the ADL index measures persons who "have difficulty with" activities of daily living, not the more restrictive ADL definition that includes only those who report "requires assistance with" activities of daily living.

9. "Formal" means purchased or provided by someone other than family and friends--either a nonprofit or for-profit agency or company.

10. Examples taken from New York City Human Resources Administration (1982).

Chapter Six

MEETING THE HOUSING NEEDS
OF THE FRAIL ELDERLY

The stakes in the effort to develop successful housing policies for the future elderly are considerable.[1] As Newman and Struyk (1987) argue, housing is a critical element in the long-term care system. Housing-based options--such as congregate housing for the frail elderly-- should be considered as an appropriate level of care for some persons in the long-term care system. Moreover, policies that assist the elderly in staying in their own homes longer should be evaluated as alternatives to more expensive care options. Increased coordination between housing and long-term care assistance is essential.

Funding for housing assistance for the elderly should be viewed in a broader federal budget context. If use of housing-based options for the frail elderly result in lower overall federal costs and reduced health expenditures in particular, then some of the savings should go to fund housing assistance. Where housing-based solutions are efficient and effective they should be expanded. For example, many of the elderly who are incapable of independent living have traditionally been served by nursing homes or similar long-term care facilities. A key characteristic of these facilities is that they provide substantial medical support to residents. Some studies suggest, however, that as much as 12 to 60 percent of the elderly living in such facilities could reside in the community if they received appropriate, primarily nonmedical, supportive services (Heumann 1985).

Projections presented in this report demonstrate that a continuation of these policies could lead to dramatic increases in the nursing home population. A larger proportion of the elderly will be very old and living alone, and fewer will have a family member who can provide care for them at home. There will be a tremendous need to conceive of ways to care for the elderly in the community for as long as possible. Policies will be required that combine social service support with housing assistance for the frail elderly. Moreover, this chapter shows that the absolute number of low-income elderly renters will increase, even though home ownership rates are expected to be high among the future elderly. Thus, there also will be an increase in the demand for affordable housing for low-income elderly persons.

There are two major dimensions of the housing issue: the cost and general quality of housing, on the one hand, and suitability for the elderly with impairments, on the other. In the past, elderly households have had higher rates of living in deficient units and of spending an inordinate share of their incomes for shelter than nonelderly households. Although today these rates for the elderly have become more similar to those of families headed by younger persons (Katsura et al. 1988), shifts in the future to more single persons and more very old households could again widen the differences, creating an expanded need for housing assistance. With respect to housing suitability, many chronically ill or frail elderly are institutionalized, at very high daily cost, who could potentially remain in the community if less costly solutions--which are also more in keeping with their preferences--were made available. A key element in such solutions is modifications to dwelling units such as ramps, grab bars, and special door and kitchen hardware that help impaired persons use their homes fully, increasing their independence and decreasing the burden on care givers.

For the more frail elderly, a variety of housing-based options have potential (Struyk et al. 1988). Examples include (1) The Congregate Housing Services Program, in which supportive services are provided to frail elderly in existing senior housing or newly constructed congregate facilities; (2) The Congregate Housing Certificate Program, in which households eligible both on the basis of low income and high risk of institutionalization would receive a voucher that would entitle them to occupy a unit in a privately operated congregate housing project that provides independent living with the necessary nonmedical support services; (3) The Housing and Support Services Certificate Program, designed as an expansion of the current rent subsidies program, in which the certificate would help low-income, frail elders not only to pay for their rent but also to pay for support services; and (4) enrollment of elderly residents of assisted housing in Social/Health Maintenance Organizations in which a single, private provider organization assumes responsibility for a full range of ambulatory, acute inpatient, nursing home, home health, and personal care services under a prospectively determined fixed budget.

This chapter reviews current housing policies that assist the elderly. Recent federal and state initiatives to assist the frail elderly are highlighted. Future needs for housing allowances for elderly renters, housing assistance for home owners, and housing for the frail elderly are outlined.

THE CURRENT SYSTEM

The main housing policies that have assisted the elderly in the past are housing assistance vouchers and their closely related counterpart, the Section 8 existing housing subsidy program.[2] These programs, only available to low-income renters, essentially help some of the elderly to afford housing with minimum quality standards. But also included within the housing assistance programs are some attempts at providing housing with supportive services to the frail elderly.

Under the housing assistance voucher program, participants find their own housing, and the federal government pays a portion of the rent. An eligible household may rent a unit meeting minimum size and quality standards for an amount less than or equal to a predetermined rent level known as the Fair Market Rent (FMR), and the federal government pays the difference between what a household can afford to pay (approximately 30 percent of adjusted gross income) and the applicable FMR. In contrast, Section 8 existing housing subsidies are tied to specific units in the existing housing stock, many of which have received other forms of aid or mortgage insurance through the Department of Housing and Urban Development (HUD). In 1988 about 1.76 million households headed by a person aged 62 or older were estimated to live in housing whose cost to the occupant has been reduced through federal subsidies (Struyk et al. 1988).

Federal housing policy has shifted considerably during the 1980s. The production-oriented approach in which the federal government backs new construction or substantial rehabilitation of units has been sharply curtailed, and assistance has moved toward the less expensive rent supplements or housing vouchers. In 1988, for example, funds were appropriated for only a small number (12,000 to 14,000) of specially designed housing units for the elderly and handicapped under the Section 202 program (Struyk et al. 1988). Hence, project-based alternatives for developing specially designed housing have been waning.

On the other hand, there has been some recent movement toward using rent supplements in more supportive living arrangements. Congress authorized two initiatives in 1983--the use of rent supplements in "single room occupancy" (SRO) housing, and the use of rent supplements in shared living arrangements. These are important indicators of more imaginative use of existing programmatic tools, although these housing arrangements do not necessarily provide the level of supportive services required by a frail elderly person.

Housing with Supportive Services

These arrangements, embodied in the housing assistance program, come in three forms, all of which involve subsidized housing projects. The first type consists of projects specially designed for use by physically impaired persons. Even if no additional services are provided, such living environments may enable people to remain in the community, although there is no hard evidence on this point. There is no accurate count of the number of such specially designed units in the subsidized inventory--an estimate is 400,000 (Newman and Struyk 1987). Persons who occupy these units do not necessarily take advantage of their special features, *because there is no requirement that such units be occupied by people with functional impairments.*

The second type of program provides supportive services to people living in government-subsidized housing (specially designed or not). At the federal level no funding for such services at the housing projects is specifically appropriated by Congress. Local agencies--housing, social, and health agencies--identify elderly people who need these services and try to arrange for them to be provided, generally using state-funded programs or programs funded by the Department of Health and Human Services. Housing projects must compete directly with other projects for the available services.

Housing projects occupied exclusively by the elderly are good "targets of opportunity" for providers of support and limited health services, because they make it easy to identify the people requiring services and increase the efficiency with which the services are delivered. Data gathered on the services available at a large sample of elderly-only public housing and Section 202 projects as part of the evaluation of the demonstration Congregate Housing Services Program suggest that such arrangements are fairly common.[3] The problem with reliance on these service providers, of course, is the uncertainty about continued funding for these services; in addition, managers of housing projects tend to accept the services available, as opposed to providing those most needed.

Finally, there are the small Congregate Housing Services Programs (CHSP). The federal CHSP program has operated in 60 public housing and Section 202 projects, with about 1,800 persons receiving supportive services under the program (Nachison 1985, p. 34). Participation is supposed to be limited to people who genuinely need the services. The service bundle has consisted of a mandatory component of twice-a-day meals and options under which services are tailored to the individual resident's needs. Probably the most distinguishing characteristic of this program is that funding for both housing assistance and supportive services comes from the Department of Housing and Urban Development (HUD), thus solving the often difficult problem of patching together funding for supportive services at the local level.

Relatively few elderly persons living in the community who require assistance with activities of daily living are served by these programs. The estimated number is between 75,000 and 135,000 elderly persons, representing between 4.9 and 8.9 percent of all elderly assisted renters (Struyk et al. 1988).

Relationship Between Housing and Long-Term Care Policy

Traditionally, housing and long-term care policies in the United States have not been coordinated formally, and even the informal linkages are tenuous. The centerpiece of involvement of the federal government in long-term care--as measured by expenditures--is the system of payments made under the Medicaid program, principally for nursing home care for people who are unable to pay for such care themselves. Under Medicaid's eligibility rules in the 1970s, some persons who needed long-term care could become eligible for it only if they entered a nursing home. Even for persons already eligible for Medicaid, nursing home care was often the only long-term care service available.

Federal legislation enacted in 1981 and 1985 began restructuring long-term care service coverage. These changes reflected a growing recognition that continued reliance on nursing home care as the primary service option is neither economically wise nor socially desirable. The new legislation allows the states--which have primary administrative responsibility for Medicaid and must share the cost of services provided--much more latitude in using community-based options to provided long-term care. This shift in emphasis away from institutional care makes housing a more important component in the overall service package.

Current law offers three ways to expand the degree of community-based services: (1) through the creative use of coverage options in the state Medicaid plans; (2) through the Section 2176 "waiver program," in which the states can apply to the Health Care Financing Administration (HCFA) for permission to substitute supportive services for institution-based services for Medicaid clients; and (3) an alternative Medicaid waiver program, Section 1915(d), which allows states to substitute supportive services for institution-based care but relaxes the requirement that states demonstrate cost-effectiveness.

Under the first option, personal care services--including meal preparation, shopping, and dressing--are covered as long as they are "medically oriented," prescribed by a physician to address a medical need, provided by a qualified provider, and supervised by a registered nurse. The principal advantage of this approach is that states can provide these services without any special permission from HCFA. As of 1984, 20 states covered some level of in-home personal care services under their Medicaid program (Burwell 1986). By far the largest of these was New York, which now spends close to $1 billion annually on personal care services for roughly 60,000 clients. In fact, New York accounts for more than three-quarters of personal care Medicaid spending. A shortage of home health providers has left the state unable to keep up with service demand.

Under the 2176 Medicaid waiver option, the primary criterion HCFA uses in judging the applications is whether the cost of providing the community-based care will be no greater than the cost for institutional services. If a waiver is granted, the states then can provide a much wider array of services and can define the target groups eligible for different types of services more flexibly than under the first option. The most common services provided are case management, homemaker services, personal care, adult day care, and rehabilitation. Some states also cover modifications to the dwelling (such as grab bars and ramps) and installation of emergency response systems. Under this option, states also have considerable latitude to determine who receives services. States can set income levels, frailty definitions (although recipients are supposed to meet the level of care criteria for nursing home admission), as well as limit service to certain areas of the state.

About 46 states have at least one waiver program in operation, but not many elderly persons are actually served under the programs. Services have not grown as one might have expected because HCFA requires states to demonstrate that *spending on waiver services is offset by at least commensurate savings to Medicaid on nursing home expenditures.* As of 1987, only a total of around 60,000 elderly and disabled persons were being served under the waiver programs nationwide (Struyk et al. 1988, p. 66).

The third Medicaid option was created in 1987 as part of the Omnibus Budget Reconciliation Act. Although this option gives states more latitude in the types of services provided and persons who could be served, states in turn must accept an indexed ceiling on federal matching for their long-term care expenditures--increases in long-term care expenditures (institutional and noninstitutional) cannot exceed 7 percent, compounded annually. This option essentially carves from Medicaid a long-term care block grant for participating states. Medicaid's institutional bias could be reduced at a state's discretion, by substantially increasing home- and community-based service spending. To date, however, only one state, Oregon, has adopted this option.

Other State Housing Initiatives for the Frail Elderly

Other state options for providing housing-based care for the elderly exist through the Supplemental Security Income (SSI) program. In addition, some states have been experimenting with congregate housing programs for the elderly.

Board and care facilities have been used as an alternative to placing the frail elderly in Intermediate Care Facilities (ICF). Board and care arrangements are favored by states because they offer a much cheaper alternative to

ICFs. Many residents receive financial assistance to live in board and care facilities through the Supplemental Security Income Program (SSI) rather than through Medicaid.

A prime example of the creative use of SSI funds in this way is New York's enriched Housing Program, operated by the state's Department of Social Services. Eligible participants receive SSI payments equivalent to those for persons in domiciliary care facilities. The program is explicitly targeted at the frail elderly, and a private nonprofit or public agency is responsible for selecting residents, securing suitable housing, and providing required services. A variety of residential settings--ranging from shared living to independent units in a congregate facility--are permitted under the program (Third Age Center 1982).

Some states have experimented with congregate housing for the elderly. Struyk and colleagues (1988) identify three models or levels of involvement that have been tried:

1. States fund a statewide service coordinator who directs housing managers to available service resources. No new services or housing are created (Minnesota and Connecticut).

2. States provide tax-exempt bond financing for the construction of congregate housing facilities. Developers are responsible for providing supportive services under loose guidelines, and the states are not involved in service provision or subsidy (Arkansas, Idaho, Illinois, Pennsylvania, North Carolina, Ohio, and Oregon).

3. States directly provide and/or subsidize the provision of new supportive services to frail elderly in existing senior housing or newly constructed congregate facilities (Connecticut, Maine, Mary-

land, Massachusetts, New Jersey, New Hampshire, New York, Vermont, and Oregon).

This third model seems to be the most appropriate for frail residents of existing assisted rental housing, people who require more support services than are currently available and who would not be able to pay for them without government assistance. As noted below, evaluations of these test cases by the Farmers Home Administration and the Administration on Aging National Demonstration of Congregate Housing for the Elderly in Rural Areas provide guidance as to the key elements in an effective system of delivering supportive services to the future frail elderly in assisted housing.

FUTURE NEEDS

The increasing number of frail elderly makes it clear that housing-based policies to assist them will be critical in the future. Policies that assist low-income renters to live in safe, healthy environments will need to continue. Moreover, those who live in these facilities and have significant health limitations should be able to get the supportive services that they need. Policies should also be considered that extend assistance to elderly, low-income home owners. Many of the elderly own their own homes but do not have the financial means to maintain them let alone to modify them so that it is possible to continue living there even with some health limitations.

In considering future policies for assisting the frail elderly to remain in the community it is useful to distinguish between housing-based and long-term-care-based options. Under the former, the package of assistance options. Under the former, the package of assistance combines supportive services with a housing-based solution. In the long-term-care-based model, housing assistance is added as necessary to community-based long-term care assistance.

Housing Allowances for Renters

Some elderly persons will continue to need help to afford safe, decent housing in the future. Although the *proportion* of elderly who rent their homes in the future is expected to decrease, the *number* of low-income renters will continue to increase. For example, table 6.1 shows that the proportion of single (never married, divorced, or widowed) elderly persons who rent their homes will decline from 38.8 percent in 1990 to 21.4 percent in 2030.[4] The steepest decline in renter rates occurs between 2010 and 2030, reflecting the composition of the elderly at that time. As noted in chapter 3, persons who are 80 years of age and older are expected to be much better off financially than preceding cohorts in this age category, as are single women retiring in 2030. Thus, they will have been more able to purchase a home than were preceding cohorts.

Table 6.2 shows the age and income characteristics of single, elderly persons who rent their homes. These projections show that renters will disproportionately fall into the lowest income quartiles, particularly in 2010 and 2030. For example, in 2010 there will be 2.4 million renters in the lowest income quartile of a total of 7.9 million elderly renters (30 percent). This effect is strongest for the very old. In 2010, for example, 37 percent of elderly renters age 80 and older fall into the lowest quarter of the income distribution (1.5 out of 4.1 million), as do 44 percent of persons age 80 and older in 2030 (1.6 million out of 3.6 million).

Table 6.1   PROJECTIONS OF SINGLE,
             ELDERLY, RENTERS, 1990-2030

Age	1990	2010	2030
Number of Persons (in thousands)			
65-69	1,337	1,248	1,282
70-79	2,816	2,541	2,848
80+	2,796	4,068	3,638
Total	6,949	7,857	7,768
Percentage of All Single Elderly Persons			
65-69	32.1	25.3	17.5
70-79	36.0	30.2	18.3
80+	46.8	40.5	27.0
Total	38.8	33.6	21.4

Source: Projections of The Urban Institute's
Dynamic Simulation of Income Model (DYNASIM),
using baseline mortality and health assumptions.

Thus, there will be an increasing number of low-income renters in the future--1.780 million in 1990, 2.365 million in 2010, and 3.075 million in 2030. More important, an increasing proportion of the low-income renters will be very old. In 2030, for example, more than half of the 3.1 million low-income renters will be at least 80 years old. These projections demonstrate the need for combining support services with low-income housing assistance for the low-income elderly. More of these persons are expected to be very old and at high risk of health limitations in the future.

Housing Assistance for Home Owners

Some attention should be given to policies that would help elderly, low-income home owners to maintain their homes, and when necessary to be able to afford improvements that would assist them to remain living there. Two possibilities include expansion of the voucher program to elderly home owners and reverse annuity mortgages.

VOUCHERS

Home owners have not been eligible to participate in housing allowance programs in the United States. The emphasis in home-ownership assistance is on helping households become home owners through subsidies embodied in the federal income tax provisions, the large program of loan interest rate write-downs administered by the Farmers Home Administration (Section 502), and the residual assistance program (Section 235) operated by the Department of Housing and Urban Development. One factor in the policy to exclude ownership from voucher eligibility may be that most elderly home owners were able to receive assistance through these various mechanisms. This is difficult to justify, however, because renter households also may have obtained housing assistance earlier in life, and yet they remain income-eligible for assistance as older persons. Another factor may be the perception that elderly home owners do not "need" subsidies because of the equity they have built up in their homes. However, there are ways to take home equity

Table 6.2   CHARACTERISTICS OF SINGLE RENTERS BY
             AGE, 1990-2030 (numbers of persons in thousands)

Age	I	II	III	IV	Total
			1990		
	($0)	($4,800)	($6,300)	($8,600)	
65-69	269	372	269	427	1,337
70-79	712	605	744	755	2,816
80+	799	842	819	336	2,796
Total	1,780	1,819	1,832	1,518	6,949
			2010		
	($0)	($6,100)	($8,600)	($12,100)	
65-69	271	246	259	472	1,248
70-79	608	648	673	612	2,541
80+	1,486	1,293	870	419	4,068
Total	2,365	2,187	1,802	1,503	7,857
			2030		
	($0)	($9,400)	($13,800)	($19,200)	
65-69	422	366	296	198	1,282
70-79	1,056	765	668	359	2,848
80+	1,597	1,191	613	237	3,638
Total	3,075	2,322	1,577	794	7,768

Source: Projections of The Urban Institute's Dynamic Simulation of
Income Model (DYNASIM) using baseline mortality and health
assumptions.

Note: Elderly single persons were divided into income quarters based
on their total projected cash income. Figures in parentheses represent
the lower income bound of the quarter.

holdings into account in determining eligibility for payments and payment levels.

Reverse Annuity Mortgages

As discussed in chapter 4, for most elderly households the equity in their home represents the majority of their net worth, and the majority of these home owners have eliminated the mortgage debt on their homes. This equity has seldom been drawn upon to support consumption, however, largely because it has been difficult to gain access to without having to sell the home. Recent initiatives to permit the elderly to use their equity for current expenses through Reverse Annuity Mortgages (RAMs) could help low-income elderly home owners to maintain their homes. The issue, of course, is whether they would choose to use their released funds to increase the quality and accessibility of their housing rather than on other items they need.

HUD typically measures housing quality in terms of structural and maintenance deficiencies and affordability. Housing modifications for the impaired are not included. As more of our population becomes older, increasing numbers of the elderly will need housing modifications if they are to continue living in the community. RAMs conceivably could be used to finance such modifications. A more certain incentive would be a voucher program to subsidize living in congregate housing. Such a voucher program could be made available to both owners and renters at time of application, as long as they meet an impairment criterion of eligibility.

Assisting the Frail Elderly

The cost of providing a satisfactory living environment for the chronically ill and frail elderly is likely to be the key housing issue for the future. As illustrated in chapter 4, as many as 16.7 million elderly persons will have some limitation in activities in daily living in 2030. This is a huge increase relative to the 1990 projection of 6.5 million persons. Promising policy options include expanding congregate housing programs and implementing programs that provide formal, in-home services to the elderly in assisted housing.

CONGREGATE HOUSING

Congregate housing offers services such as meal plans, transportation, housekeeping, and recreation. Thus, congregate housing facilities can foster independent living by persons who otherwise might enter institutions. Furthermore, congregate housing appears less expensive than long-term care facilities for comparable levels of service. Heumann (1985) estimated that congregate facilities are about one-third less expensive than long-term care facilities.

It has been difficult to prove that the congregate housing programs attempted so far are cost-effective. The key stumbling block, as revealed by a series of experimental programs, has been an inability to define the target population correctly. Even though programs have applied strict disability criteria in determining eligibility for community-based services, persons with severe functional impairments are still at relatively low risk of institutional placement. Some combination of informal and formal services is sufficient to keep them at home. One effective way to identify people who are at risk is to draw recipients of these services from applicants for admission to nursing homes. Although this screening device may seem extreme, it is the only one that has proven effective to date.

This finding clearly has implications for housing programs that are being designed to provide cost-effective services to the frail elderly. We already noted the poor results in this area of the Congregate Housing Services Program, in part because of inadequate screening of the recipient population. The so-called targeting issue certainly will have to be addressed in designing new housing initiatives.

One measure of success of the Congregate Housing Services Program is whether it effectively delayed the necessity of institutional placement for program participants. It has not been shown conclusively that congregate housing affects institutionalization rates. An evaluation of the Congregate Housing Services Program (CHSP) discovered that by the end of the demonstration period there was no significant difference in the rate at which participants and controls were permanently placed in institutions, but there was a difference in the lengths of stays between the two groups (Sherwood et al. 1984, Table IV.2). Participants in the project were more likely to be institutionalized for shorter periods.

Some argue that the success of Congregate Housing Services Programs could be enhanced if the population served by the program is restricted to people who are vulnerable to institutionalization (Newman and Struyk 1987). This targeting issue seems to be foremost in importance. Several factors are important. First, evaluation of prospective participants must be trained and given clear guidance on the degree of impairment that constitutes sufficient severity to warrant admission. A key point in this area is the great need for more research to define accurate predictors of risk of institutionalization and corresponding assessment tools for local use. Given current knowledge, a reasonable standard that could be implemented consistently is the presence of at least one activity of daily living (ADL) limitation severe enough to require personal assistance and one or more instrumental activity of daily living (IADL) limitations. Using a centralized screening system at the local level, rather than having staff at each project conduct their own assessments, is preferable because it permits more consistent application of guidelines in a process that inevitably requires judgments. In general, improvements in targeting and screening increase both the likelihood of savings from delayed institutionalization and the willingness of states to participate.

Second, careful case management and tailoring of services are central to any cost containment effort and to effectively meeting the individual needs of participants. The skills of the on-site coordinator and regular contact with the coordinator, as at mealtimes, are important in this regard. Formal client evaluation and modification of the service package should be repeated at least annually after admission into the program. Moreover, copayments from participants, based on income and on the quantity of services received, are advisable; both offset program costs and help contain service use.

Third, a core package of nonmedical services should be offered at each facility, but mandatory participation in a service is justifiable only when economies of scale in its provision outweigh tailoring considerations, as may be so with congregate meal service. A higher level of services (including medical services) that can be offered by congregate programs could be arranged through state Medicaid offices using waivered home and community-based service options.

Fourth, in terms of tailoring and avoidance of overservicing, there are strong arguments for providing cash payments to housing providers with which to purchase services from vendors or to deliver them directly, rather than forcing projects to broker in-kind services from several sources that are funded directly by a variety of state agencies. Unifying the sources of funds to the provider into a single payment would simplify management and coordination tasks. In the case of federally assisted housing, channeling the funds through a single federal agency is appropriate. These changes would leave coordinators freer to fit services specifically to client needs and to provide needed services themselves, where appropriate, or to purchase them from vendors offering a less expensive quality product.

Fifth, agency oversight would be essential for ensuring the quality and adequacy of services. Thorough supervision may necessitate cooperation between the federal agency's area offices and state social service agencies. Such oversight becomes particularly important when housing projects have greater responsibility for providing service. Oversight would be facilitated by channeling funds to a single agency, because the agency then would have firm information on each project's resources.

PROVIDING SERVICES TO ELDERLY IN ASSISTED HOUSING

Several possible new approaches show promise for serving frail elderly residents of assisted housing. They include the Housing and Support Services Certificate Program, Social/Health Maintenance Organizations, and the Congregate Housing Certificate Program.

Under the Housing Support Services Certificate Program (HSSCP), frail elders who were determined eligible by the administering agent (the local housing authority or a nonprofit organization, possibly including a current sponsor in the Section 202 program) would receive a certificate covering the costs of support services. The payments for services would be used by the local administering agent to provide case management and the necessary support services, either directly or through various vendors. In principle, the agent could contract out the whole case management and service delivery responsibility. The agent also could contract with several vendors and allow households to select among them. HSSCP has yet to be implemented.

Four Social/Health Maintenance Organizations (S/HMOs) have been in operation on a demonstration basis since 1985. Under this model, a single private provider organization assumes responsibility for a full range of ambulatory, acute inpatient, nursing home, home health, and personal care services under a prospectively determined fixed budget (capitation payment, similar to an HMO). All elderly residents of assisted housing in a locality would be encouraged to enroll in an S/HMO that then would be wholly responsible for managing cases and for tailoring and providing services to clients. The residents' monthly capitated enrollment fees would be subsidized in whole or in part.

Under the Congregate Housing Certificate Program (CHCP), which exists only in concept and is similar to the last option considered above as a potential housing policy for the future, households eligible on the basis of low income and high risk of institutionalization would receive a certificate entitling them to occupy a unit in a congregate housing project that provides independent living with the necessary nonmedical support services. The voucher would cover the cost of both housing and the level of support services warranted, with the households contributing 50 to 60 percent of their incomes toward the combined costs. As proposed, vouchers could be used at approved privately operated facilities.

These options represent several of many that could be developed from basic building blocks designed to improve targeting, control costs, and improve tailoring of services to match needs. The amount of responsibility assigned to agencies versus that given to individual elderly persons for securing services, the extent of integration of payments for housing and support services, and the application of and approach to existing housing programs all could be varied. The models presented are good examples of what could be done.

Notes, chapter six

1. This chapter was adapted from several recent papers published by The Urban Institute: Newman and Struyk (1987); Struyk et al. (1988); and Katsura, Struyk, and Newman (1988).

2. For a detailed comparison of HUD's voucher program and its similar Section 8 existing housing subsidy program, see Kennedy and Finkel (1987).

3. Section 202 projects are specially designed housing developed by nonprofit sponsors for occupancy by elderly households and households with a physically handicapped member. Federal subsidies are provided in the form of direct loans that carry below-market interest rates and, in recent years, through rental assistance payments that are available under the Section 9 program for all occupants who are eligible to receive them.

4. Numbers are not shown for elderly married persons because most of them are expected to be home owners.

REFERENCES

Aaron, Henry J. 1986. "When is a Burden Not a Burden? The Elderly in America." *The Brookings Review* 4 (Summer): 17-24.

Andrews, Emily. 1985. *The Changing Profile of Pensions in America*. Washington D.C.: Employee Benefit Research Institute.

Baldwin, Leo. 1985. *Home Equity Conversion*. Washington, D.C.: American Association of Retired Persons.

Beller, Daniel. 1986. "Coverage and Vesting Status in Private Pension Plans, 1972-1983." In *The Handbook of Pension Statistics, 1985*. Office of Pension and Welfare Benefit Programs, U.S. Department of Labor, Chicago, Illinois: Commerce Clearing House, Inc.

Bloom, David E., and Neil G. Bennett. 1985. *Marriage Patterns in the United States*. National Bureau of Economic Research Working Paper no. 1701. Cambridge, Mass: National Bureau of Economic Research.

Board of Trustees, Federal Old-Age and Survivors Insurance and Disability Insurance Trust Funds. 1986. *The 1986 Annual Report*. Washington, D.C.: Social Security Administration.

Boskin, Michael J. 1977. "Social Security and Retirement Decisions." *Economic Inquiry* 15 (1): 1-25.

Burkhauser, Richard V. 1979. "The Pension Acceptance Decision of Older Workers." *Journal of Human Resources* 14 (Winter): 63-75.

Burkhauser, Richard V., and Greg J. Duncan. 1988. "Life Events, Public Policy, and the Economic Vulnerability of Children and the Elderly." In *The Vulnerable*, ed. John Palmer, Timothy Smeeding, and Barbara Torrey. Washington, D.C.: Urban Institute Press.

Burt, Martha R., and Karen J. Pittman. 1985. *Testing the Social Safety Net*. Washington, D.C.: Urban Institute Press.

Burtless, Gary, and Jerry Hausman. 1980. "Individual Retirement Decisions Under an Employer-Provided Pension Plan and Social Security." Unpublished paper (November).

Burtless, Gary, and Robert Moffitt. 1984. "The Effect of Social Security Benefits on the Labor Supply of the Aged." In *Retirement and Economic Behavior*, ed. Henry J. Aaron and Gary Burtless. Washington, D.C.: Brookings Institution.

Burwell, Brian. 1986. "Home and Community-Based Care Options Under Medicaid." In *Affording Access to Quality Care*. Washington, D.C.: National Governors' Association.

Capitman, John. 1984. *Supplemental Report on Adult Day Health Care Program in California: A Comparative Cost Analysis*. Sacramento: California Department of Public Services.

Carpenter, David R. 1989. "Old Age Illnesses Needn't Bankrupt Americans." *The Generational Journal* 2 (April): 86-87.

Carter, Gene. 1983. "Private Pensions: 1982 Legislation." *The Social Security Bulletin* 46 (August): 3-8.

Chapman, Steven H., Mitchell P. LaPlante, and Gail Wilensky. 1986. "Life Expectancy and Health Status of the Aged." *Social Security Bulletin* 46 (October): 24-48.

Clark, Robert, and Thomas Johnson. 1980. *Retirement in the Dual Career Family.* Final Report SSA Grant no. 10-P-90453-4-02, June.

Congressional Budget Office. 1987. *Tax Policy for Pensions and Other Retirement Saving.* Washington, D.C.: U.S. Government Printing Office.

Danziger, Sheldon, Robert Haveman, and Robert Plotnick. 1981. "How Income Transfer Programs Affect Work, Savings, and the Income Distribution: A Critical Review." *Journal of Economic Literature* 19 (September): 975-1028.

Economic Report of the President. 1989. Washington, D.C.: U.S. Government Printing Office.

Dawson, Deborah, Gerry Hendershot, and John Fulton. 1987. "Aging in the Eighties: Functional Limitations of Individuals Age 65 Years and Over." Advance Data from the Vital Statistics of the National Center for Health Statistics, no. 133, June 10.

Doty, Pamela, Korbin Liu, and Joshua Wiener. 1985. "An Overview of Long-Term Care." *Health Care Financing Review* 6 (Spring): 69-78.

Fields, Gary S., and Olivia S. Mitchell. 1984a. *Retirement, Pensions, and Social Security.* Cambridge. MA: MIT Press.

_____. 1984b. "The Effects of Social Security Reforms on Retirement Ages and Retirement Incomes." *Journal of Public Economics* 25 (November): 143-59.

Findlay, Steven. 1989. "Paying for Long-Term Health Care Insurance." *The Generational Journal,* 2 (April): 65-66.

Fries, James F. 1983. "The Compression of Morbidity." *Milbank Memorial Fund Quarterly/Health and Society* 61(3): 397-419.

_____. 1980. "Aging, Natural Death, and the Compression of Morbidity." *New England Journal of Medicine* 30 (3): 130-35.

Gaberlavage, George. 1987. *Social Services to Older Persons Under the Social Services Block Grant.* Washington, D.C.: Public Policy Institute, American Association of Retired Persons.

Grad, Susan. 1988. *Income of the Population 55 or Older, 1986.* Washington, D.C.: U.S. Department of Health and Human Services, Social Security Administration, June.

Greenwood, Daphne T., and Edward N. Wolff. 1988. "Related Wealth Holdings of Children and the Elderly in the United States, 1962-1983." In *The Vulnerable,* eds. John Palmer, Timothy Smeeding, and Barbara Torrey. Washington, D.C.: Urban Institute Press.

Gruenberg, Ernest M. 1977. "The Failures of Success." *Milbank Memorial Fund Quarterly/Health and Society* 55 (Winter): 3-24.

Gustman, Alan L., and Thomas L. Steinmeier. 1985. "The 1983 Social Security Reforms and Labor Supply Adjustments of Older Individuals in the Long Run." *Journal of Labor Economics* 3(2): 237-53.

_____. 1984. "Partial Retirement and the Analysis of Retirement Behavior." *Industrial and Labor Relations Review* 37 (April): 403-15.

Hacker, Scott, and Timothy McBride. 1989. *The Dynamic Simulation of Income Model, Vol. III: The Cross-Section Imputation Model.* Washington, D.C.: Urban Institute.

Health Care Financing Administration. 1988. "National Health Expenditures, 1987-2000." *Health Care Financing Review* 10 (Spring): 119.

Heumann, L. 1985. *A Cost Comparison of Congregate Housing and Long-Term Care Facilities in Mid-West.* Urbana, Illinois: University of Illinois, Housing Research and Development Program.

Holahan, John, and Korbin Liu. 1988. "Long-Term Care: Past Policies and Future Prospects." Working Paper 1616-01. Washington, D.C.: Urban Institute, September.

Ippolito, Richard, and Walter Kolodrubetz. 1986. *The Handbook of Pension Statistics.* Chicago: Commerce Clearing House.

Jacobs, Bruce. 1985. "The National Potential of Home Equity Conversion." University of Rochester Working Paper 8502.

Jacobs, Bruce, and William Weissert. 1984. "Home Equity Financing of Long-Term Care for the Elderly." University of North Carolina, January.

Johnson, Jon, and Sheila Zedlewski. 1989. *The Dynamic Simulation of Income Model, Vol. II (revised)*. Washington, D.C.: Urban Institute.

Katsura, Harold, Raymond J. Struyk, and Sandra J. Newman. 1989. *Housing for the Elderly in 2010: Projections and Policy Options*. Washington, D.C.: Urban Institute Press.

Katz, S., T.D. Downs, H.R. Cash, and R.C. Grotz. 1970. "Progress in the Development of the Index of ADL." *The Gerontologist* 10(1): 20-30.

Kennedy, S., and M. Finkel. 1987. *Report of First Year Findings for the Freestanding Housing Voucher Demonstration*. Washington, D.C.: U.S. Department of Housing and Urban Development.

King, Miriam. 1988. *Changes in the Living Arrangements of the Elderly: 1960-2030*. Washington D.C.: Congressional Budget Office, March.

Kotlikoff, Lawrence, and Daniel Smith. 1983. *Pensions in the American Economy*. Chicago: University of Chicago Press.

Kramer, M. 1980. "The Rising Pandemic of Mental Disorders and Associated Chronic Diseases and Disabilities." *Acta Psychiatrica Scandanavica Supplement* 285 (3): 62.

Lesnoy, Selig D., and Dean R. Leimer. 1985. "Social Security and Private Saving: Theory and Historical Evidence." *Social Security Bulletin* 48 (January): 14-30.

Liu, Korbin, and Elizabeth S. Cornelius. 1988. "ADLs and Eligibility for Long-Term Care Services." Report prepared for the Commonwealth Fund Commission on Elderly People Living Alone. Washington, D.C.: Urban Institute.

Manton, Kenneth. 1986. "Past and Future Life Expectancy Increases at Later Ages: Their Implications for the Linkage of Chronic Morbidity, Disability and Mortality." *Journal of Gerontology* 41(5): 672-81.

Michel, Richard C., and Frank S. Levy. 1988. *Will Baby Boomers Live as Well as Their Parents?* Washington, D.C.: Urban Institute.

Mitchell, Olivia, and Gary S. Fields. 1982. "The Effect of Pensions and Earnings on Retirement: A Review Essay." In *Research in Labor Economics, Vol. 5,* ed. Ronald G. Ehrenberg. Greenwich, CT: JAI Press.

Nachison, J. 1985. "Congregate Housing for the Low and Moderate Income Elderly--A Needed Federal State Partnership." *Journal of Housing for the Elderly* 3 (Fall/Winter): 65-80.

National Center for Health Statistics. 1988. *Vital Statistics of the United States, 1984, Vol. III, Marriage and Divorce.* DHHS Pub. No. (PHS) 88-1103, Public Health Service. Washington, D.C.: U.S. Government Printing Office.

_____. 1984. *Vital Statistics of the United States, 1979, Vol. I, Natality*. Washington, D.C.: U.S. Government Printing Office.

Newman, Sandee, and Raymond Struyk. 1987. *Housing and Supportive Services: Federal Policy for the Frail Elderly and Chronically Mentally Ill*. Urban Institute Paper 2199-01A. Washington, D.C.: Urban Institute.

New York City Human Resources Administration. 1982. *Adult Protective Services: The State of the Art*. New York: Human Resources Administration.

Quinn, Joseph F., Richard V. Burkhauser, and Daniel A. Myers. 1989. *Passing The Torch: The Influence of Economic Incentives on Work and Retirement*. Kalamazoo, MI: The Upjohn Institute for Employment Research.

Radner, Daniel B. 1988. "Net Worth and Financial Assets of Age Groups in 1984." *The Social Security Bulletin* 51 (March): 4-26.

_____. 1987. "Money Incomes of Aged and Nonaged Family Units, 1967-84." *The Social Security Bulletin* 50(8): 9-28.

Rivlin, Alice M., and Joshua M. Wiener. 1988. *Caring for the Disabled Elderly: Who Will Pay?* Washington, D.C.: Brookings Institution.

Rosenfeld, Carl, and Scott Campbell Brown. 1979. "The Labor Force Status of Older Workers." *Monthly Labor Review* 102 (November): 27-31.

Sammartino, Frank. 1987. "The Effect of Health on Retirement." *Social Security Bulletin* 50 (February): 31-47.

_____. 1982. "The Timing of Social Security Acceptance by Older Men: Examining the Financial Incentives." Technical Analysis Paper no. 24, Office of the Assistant Secretary for Planning and Evaluation, U.S. Department of Health and Human Services, January.

Scholen, Kenneth. 1985. *An Overview of Home Equity Conversion Plans.* Washington, D.C.: The National Center for Home Equity Conversion.

Schwartz, Saul, Sheldon Danziger, and Eugene Smolensky. 1984. "The Choice of Living Arrangements by the Elderly." In *Retirement and Economic Behavior,* ed. Henry J. Aaron and Gary Burtless. Washington, D.C.: Brookings Institution.

Sherman, Sally. 1985. "Reported Reasons Retired Workers Left Their Last Job: Findings from the New Beneficiary Survey." *Social Security Bulletin* 48 (March): 22-30.

Sherwood, S., S.A. Morris, and E. Bernstein. 1984. *Targeting and Tailoring Performance of the Congregate Housing Services Program.* Boston: Department of Social Gerontological Research, Hebrew Rehabilitation Center for Aged.

Soldo, B.J., M. Sharma, and R.T. Campbell. 1984. "Determinants of Community Living Arrangements of Older Unmarried Women." *Journal of Gerontology* 39(2): 492-98.

Stecker, Margaret L. 1951. "Beneficiaries Prefer to Work." *Social Security Bulletin* 14 January.

Storey, James, Richard Michel, and Sheila Zedlewski. 1984. *Saving Social Security: The Short- and Long-Run Effects of the 1983 Amendments.* Washington, D.C.: Urban Institute.

Struyk, Raymond, Douglas B. Page, Sandra Newman, Marcia Carroll, Makiko Ueno, Barbara Cohen, and Paul Wright. 1988. *Providing Supportive Services to Frail Elderly in Federally Assisted Housing*. Washington, D.C.: Urban Institute Press.

Svahn, John A. and Mary Ross. 1983. "Social Security Amendments of 1983: Legislative History and Summary of Provisions." *Social Security Bulletin* 46 (July): 3-48.

Third Age Center. 1982. *An Evaluation of an Innovative Program for Older Persons Sponsored by the New York Department of Social Services*. New York: New York Department of Social Services.

U.S. Bureau of the Census. 1987. *Statistical Abstract of the United States: 1988 (108th edition)*. Washington, D.C.: U.S. Government Printing Office.

———. 1984. *Projections of the Population of the United States, by Age, Sex, and Race: 1983 to 2080*. Washington D.C.: U.S. Government Printing Office.

———. 1976. *Statistical Abstract of the United States: 1976 (97th edition)*. Washington, D.C.: U.S. Government Printing Office.

U.S. Congress, House Committee on Ways and Means. 1989. *Background Material and Data on Programs Within the Jurisdiction of the Committee on Ways and Means*. Washington, D.C.: U.S. Government Printing Office/ Committee Print, March.

U.S. Congress, Senate Special Committee on Aging. 1986. *Developments in Aging*. Washington, D.C.: U.S. Government Printing Office.

_____. 1985. *How Older Americans Live: An Analysis of Census Data.* Washington, D.C.: U.S. Government Printing Office.

U.S. Public Health Service. 1976. *Fertility Tables for Birth Cohorts by Color, United States, 1917-1973.* Washington, D.C.: U.S. Government Printing Office.

Wade, Alice. 1988. "Social Security Area Population Projections: 1987." *Social Security Bulletin* 51 (February): 3-30.

Wertheimer, Richard, and Sheila Zedlewski. 1984. *The Dynamic Simulation of Income Model, Volume I.* Washington, D.C.: Urban Institute.

Wister, A. V., and T. K. Burch. 1983. "Living Arrangement Choices Among the Elderly." *Canadian Journal on Aging* 4 (3) 127-44.

Wolf, Douglas. 1984. "Kin Availability and the Living Arrangements of Older Women." *Social Science Research* 13 (April): 72-89.

Wolf, Douglas, and Beth Soldo. 1988. "Household Composition Choices of Older Unmarried Women." *Demography* 25 (August): 387-405.

Ycas, Martynas. 1987. "Recent Trends in Health Near the Age of Retirement: New Findings from the Health Interview Survey." *The Social Security Bulletin* 50 (February): 5-30.

Zedlewski, Sheila R. 1990. "The Development of the Dynamnic Simulation of Income Model (DYNASIM)." In *Microsimulation Techniques for Tax and Transfer Analysis*, ed. Gordon H. Lewis and Richard C. Michel. Urban Institute Press, Washington, D.C.